I would like to extend my gratitude to my colleagues who shared their time and their stories, the professionals who helped me by transcribing, editing, and creating some beautiful artwork.

Most of all, I appreciate my family and am thankful they believe in me and support this project. My husband, Bill, listened to endless conversation and brainstormed with me, tolerating my long hours on the computer. I have a special thank-you for my dear Aunt Polly, the Editor-in-Chief, who oversaw the final product and ensured a better understanding of the field by expanding the Glossary. Many thanks to Diane Reppun for all of her help, technical expertise, advice and friendship.

ISBN 978-0-9798411-0-1

1st edition
WJT Bashamer Publishing
10156 Camberley Lane
Cupertino, CA 95014
ourhrsite.com

Cover Design: Mark Brown Digital Arts
markbrowndigitalarts.com
First Edit: Chandler Harris
harris.chandler.googlepages.com/writenow2
Editor in Chief: Polly Liss
Transcription: Transcription Institute   transcriptioninstitute.com

Printed in the United States of America.

INTRODUCTION

Have you ever wondered about the people whose job it is to fill openings at companies? I work in Human Resources in the Silicon Valley, and when presenting career workshops, I discovered that few people knew there were various types of recruiters. There are a wide variety of recruiting skills and specialties, and some job seekers believe all they need to do is contact a recruiter and that person will find them a job. It doesn't work that way!

Discussing careers with friends and colleagues in the field revealed that many entered recruiting in a circuitous way – it was not their first choice of a profession. Recruiting seems to be one of those wonderful "accidental" careers.

The recruiters interviewed for this book discussed their career paths, some of their techniques, tips for potential recruiters and useful information for job seekers in general. It was exciting and interesting to interview my colleagues and provide the opportunity for them to share their stories with you.

My website provides articles and books regarding life, love and work. If there is an occupation you'd like to read about or a person you feel would be of interest to others, please contact me at mstein@ourhrsite.com or visit me on the web at ourhrsite.com.

I'm just a click away.

Marcia

SHARE YOUR STORY

I'd enjoy hearing from you about this book. What did you enjoy most? How did these stories affect you? Did you gain information for your career path or did you learn how to work with recruiters in a different way?

You're also invited to share your stories with me. If accepted, your story or suggestion may be published either as an individual article or as part of a new book. You can send your suggestion along with your complete contact information to mstein@ourhrsite.com, or you can see my form on the website at www.ourhrsite.com.

It's been a real pleasure interviewing these professionals and I hope you enjoy reading about their paths.

TABLE OF CONTENTS

	Introduction	i
	Share Your Story	ii
I	Sourcers	1
II	Contract Recruiters	25
III	Staffing Directors	93
IV	Executive (Retained) Search	115
	Glossary	130
	Resources	133
	About Marcia Stein	134
	Request Form	135

1

SOURCERS

oelle Tardieu
Noelle has experience in software quality assurance and has worked at an employment agency. Her technical background, curiosity and interest in people have led to a dynamic position as a sourcer and recruiter at Yahoo! in Sunnyvale, California.

Noelle: I've been at Yahoo! over four years working as a Specialist Talent Scout, often referred to as a sourcer. I'm great at finding talent and I've worked at almost every part of Yahoo!: Finance, G&A [General and Administration], Marketing, Sales, Executive, Exec Admin and now I'm in Engineering. Basically they put me on when they have a fire – meaning that there's a problem area or something's happened and they need help. Right now I'm doing a full recruiter job and sourcing because what they need is candidates. So many recruiters have gotten to the point where all they want to do is the process and maybe a little bit of account management, but they forget the whole thing is about flow – it's about getting good candidates into the process. That's what I do; I try to find candidates that are not on job boards. My thing is teaching – I did a training yesterday – and it's all about the different tools that sourcers have and this continues to evolve. Now we can actually create customized search engines for ourselves – sourcers here do this and it is evolving into new areas. It's just amazing. You never know it all when it comes to sourcing. You continually learn more and more and I love that.

Marcia: Tell me how you got into recruiting.

Noelle: I started out in Tech Support and went into QA [quality assurance]. I was in QA for almost 15 years. I was at Apple for 10 years and I was at Symantec where I specialized in graphic applications. I loved talking to the beta test sites and I loved all that stuff. For years people would say, "Oh, you should be in sales, you should be in marketing with your personality." But I was a single mom and my son has special needs and I needed a job where I was mostly working 9 to 5. Once in a while there was some overtime, but usually it was a very straight kind of thing. It wasn't until my son moved out where I said I'm ready for something new. I'd taken a Myers-Briggs test at a career evaluation at Claris. The person doing the training kind of whispered in my ear, "Have you ever thought about recruiting?" I'd never even thought about it. "You're an ENFP; you'd be a great recruiter." ["ENFP" refers to a personality type revealed through the Myers-Briggs Indicator.]

I thought, wow, I should look into this and I did. I had just started a project; it was Claris Works for kids and it ended up being education product of the year. It was going to be probably about a two-year project and I really wanted to finish it and I liked my team. There's a thing about engineering – you're part of a team, you have a commitment and you want to finish the project.

I started volunteering at recruiting events and reaching out and they used to say, "Why do you want to do this?" I said I just wanted to check it out. The more I looked into it, the more I liked it. The part that was great about QA was the investigative, finding the tools and getting that gem, that bug or that great candidate. So, it sort of did fit in my profile. I quit my job in '97 and took a $30,000 a year recruiting job. I had just gotten married and I said this is my chance to do a career I really want to do. My son was in a good situation and I did it and never looked back.

Marcia: What kind of recruiting job was it?

Noelle: It was an agency recruiting job. I went to work for this woman, Lisa Pisacane; she's absolutely brilliant. She took a chance on me and I learned everything from her. The first year I doubled my salary from what I made as a QA person. But it wasn't about the money - I took to it like a duck to water.

Marcia: Did she teach you about finding candidates or finding job orders, or everything simultaneously?

Noelle: Yes, Lisa showed me how she successfully sourced. I also used some of my QA bug finding skills. I brought in Adobe, 3Com and others. I also had several contractors on the books. I made a half million dollars for them the first year, which is not too bad in 1997. After Lisa left the company, the new leadership kept saying, "Every year we want you to double your numbers." I was already working long hours the second year– really pretty hard – and I said, I can't double my output. I had some great people on contract and high fill rates. I worked for Lisa again when I went to an Internet startup.

Marcia: What do you think was the key to your success?

Noelle: I had a really great leader/mentor in Lisa. She's absolutely one of those people that are genuinely great and ethical, too. She is nice from the first call to the last call of the day. I learned a lot from her. I had that whole sourcing piece –I just developed that part. Then I went to work for a startup and I was there for a couple of years and my goal was to get into an IPO [Initial Public Offering] and I did. I helped them hire 250 really good people.

What I realized is in recruiting you have all this process stuff that takes you away from the fun stuff and for me that was the sourcing – that became clear. I went back to Apple as a recruiter but I realized sourcing was beginning to become a different area. In some companies it was still a coordinator; it hadn't come to the level that it is now at Yahoo! where recruiters and sourcers are on the same level playing field. I just really keyed in on that and it became a focus for me. When I came here they said, "We want you to come and help us with the sourcing – this is a new thing for us." Another guy and I were hired at the same time just to do sourcing; he was the telephone guy. You always have to have some phone, but I was both. I mean, Internet was just using the search and the development of candidates.

Marcia: How do you find the latest search tools or the latest ways to find people on the Internet?

Noelle: Sometimes it's using tools that we've had before but they've evolved, but I think that there's never one particular thing. I heard today that (Company X) only uses LinkedIn – nothing else, not even job boards any more -which is incredible. LinkedIn could be bought tomorrow and then what are you going to do?

Marcia: You're also knocking out millions of people who are not on LinkedIn.

Noelle: Exactly. I think that great sourcing has to include name sourcing. There is a gaping hole to candidates and that is via phone systems – you have to pick up the phone and call and they have phone directories after hours. If you ask people, "Can you help me?" people are going to help you. You tell who you're with, "I'm searching for …, can you help me with this?" Fifty percent of the time people will say yes. You get information that nobody else has.

That's just one thing, but sourcing is tools. It's sort of like parenting; you have different parenting techniques and tools. It's never the same thing. I used to have on my kitchen cupboard all these lists of parenting tools. OK, which one do I need now? It is the same thing with sourcing. There're all these different tools and it's never going to be the same tools and there's got to be a strategy. Don't get bogged down with one thing.

Sometimes I can get into a place where I'm sourcing and I've found a great spot and I'm just taking this information and I'm putting it aside to look at it. It's like programming almost: I see it like that. You get to a spot and you cannot stop, because it took you a long way to get yourself into this location and you want to harvest all that information. I'll look up and it's dark, around 7 pm and I've been sitting for four hours, my legs ache, my shoulders ache, but I have all this great information.

Marcia: And you're excited about it.

Noelle: I'm excited about it, but I feel bad with my body crunched up but that's how it is. You find great stuff and you put it all aside and then you can go back and see how good this is.

Marcia: Recruiters who've been around for a while have seen ups and downs in the economy. We can have periods of time where recruiters are out of work for two or three years or however long it takes.

Noelle: I went through it – yeah.

Marcia: How did you plan for that and how did you get through it?

Noelle: It's hard to plan for those things, but you're right, we all knew the Internet bubble was going to break eventually. I've talked to people who've been in the business and they'll say it's either job order driven or candidate driven. When the economy is down it's totally job-order driven. During that tough time, what I did was sourcing on different projects for people. I worked on contingency. I realized that when you're only in high tech you're more vulnerable. When that happens again, because it will – there are highs and lows of the economy – I think what I would do is go into names sourcing and work for different areas and not just high tech. Ms. X does that kind of work and makes, on her own, a half a million a year doing that, even in down times and she has people that work for her that do it. Her income is probably way over a million and it's like $42 a name and that's what she does, just names sourcing. If you're really great at what you do, I don't think you have to worry too much. I've developed my skills more – I used that time to really take my sourcing to a whole new level.

I ran into Cheryl, who's a VP here, at an event. And she said, "What are you doing?" I said I have just taken sourcing and made it a specialty – I see where companies need to have that. A couple of months later I heard she was at Yahoo! I called to congratulate her and she called me a few weeks later and said, "Can you come in for an interview for a sourcing job?"

Marcia: So it's through that network.

Noelle: That networking – yeah. And she's still here.

Marcia: What do you think makes a good recruiter?

Noelle: If you're going to be in jobs where a recruiter does not have a sourcer, you have to know how to find candidates. It makes you much more valuable. I think that great people skills, intuition, knowing people and, when meeting somebody, having that intuition that says there's something more behind the words that this person's not telling me makes you a good recruiter. You really have to understand people on many levels. It takes all your senses to be a recruiter. You pick up things by talking to people and you have to use that in your recruiting. Sometimes you have to have a lot of empathy; people tell you things because this is their livelihood. I think that you have to have some sales. You have to believe in what you're selling, because you're taking somebody from a company that is supporting their family. You have to believe in the company you're selling, because that's nothing to muck around with – somebody's livelihood – their family and how many other people here or in other countries are relying on that person's money for their existence. I think you really have to believe in that.

I don't believe that you should come in and try to low-ball somebody, just to get them on board and it looks good for your numbers. I really believe you have to give honest and fair offers and don't play salary games. Do the best you can for somebody -- I really believe in that. Be straight, authentic, and genuine. People appreciate that. As a recruiter you have to sometimes help the person that is a really good candidate but their resume doesn't show it. Take some time to tell them how to do it. I never will fix a resume for anybody, but I will tell people how to fix their resumes.

I think as a recruiter we have an obligation to give back to the community and that means sometimes helping people when it's not going to come back and pad your pocket. There're times you have to help people and be honest with somebody. "Let me just give you some feedback. In this interview, you spent the whole time talking, not listening." Or, "In this interview you didn't show any interest or motivation for the job. Now you're telling me you want the job, but you needed to show that in the interview." I think we have to be able to be honest and tell people that. Let's say you come across somebody that didn't do well in an interview, but you could say, "Here's some advice I can give you. You didn't want to change your resume, but here's the way you can get more interviews." People don't realize that resume styles change and come and go and by making a few changes on a resume, you could make yourself more marketable. Your resume's a marketing brochure for yourself and people don't know how to do that sometimes. Here at Yahoo! we get thousands of resumes a month.

Marcia: How do you stand out if you're one of thousands?

Noelle: You stand out by putting in your resume your major accomplishments that you're most proud about at every job. Resumes are like fashion: resume styles evolve, so stay up on resume style trends. Currently, resumes are all about accomplishments and not a laundry list of duties. Resume verbs are important too.

Be 110 percent honest. If you don't have a degree, don't put it on there. We hire people without degrees, so don't lie about that. If you're an unethical person, I would say look at that because people want people that have character and ethics. Especially here it's very important - they just drive that home here. Be honest about what you haven't done, but write down your accomplishments: how you made money, saved money, saved time. People want to know that. "Oh, they saved money? Saved time? Made money? We could use that person," because hiring is about solving a problem. There's a problem over there; we need to find an integration person – whatever.

7

Marcia: You have to quantify.

Noelle: Yeah! And if you're an engineer, write what your role was. What was the operating system platform? If you're a marketing person, you created an e-mail campaign – if you don't write what happened, how am I supposed to guess what was the result of that campaign. If you developed a new application, was it on time? Was it successful? What was your role? What was the scope? People leave those things out. I can't always help people, but once in a while somebody refers you to somebody and you say, "I could help you." You know they could make some changes and be successful. If they can't get a job here, they're going to get more interviews at other places.

Marcia: If someone were to say, "I'm thinking about a career in recruiting," do you have some advice for that person?

Noelle: I think it's a great career. I would say make sure that you have the skills – the gifts, the values – all of those things. If you're just thinking that this is a way to make a fast buck, this is not the career. I think in recruiting there are the dumpster-diving recruiters and the sourcers that want to go buy names, or want to get behind a security guard at a company and those that lie on the phone – those kind of people we really don't want in recruiting. We really want people that really have that investigative interest; they love to find stuff and they get joy from that. They're passionate about this kind of work. It's a great career.

It's different every day and you have to prioritize your work on the fly. There're days you're going to have highs, where three candidates signed the offer, they love the job and they're ready to go. There're other days the candidate is going to take another offer and you have to start all over. You don't have a back-up candidate and you have to kind of prepare yourself for the highs and lows. If you're going to be a recruiter, you really have to have the sourcing side, because you're going to end up in jobs where you don't have a sourcer. Unfortunately, there are recruiters that do not know how to source or have any desire to do that.

8

Marcia: Is there some place they could go to learn that?

Noelle: There are some really good books. I really like Barbara Ling; she has some very good books on sourcing. People who've been librarians are often very good sourcers. You don't have to be an extrovert, but you have to be able to stretch your introverted self if you're going to be a recruiter; extroverts seem to do a little better. They love finding things.

If you go to SCIP.org (Society for Competitive Intelligence), they have some very good books about how competitive intelligence really works in recruiting. You have to know your industry – what's happening, why are they unhappy at competitor XYZ? What's happening at that company? Oh, I see they've cut back on benefits or the focals [review how performance matches the goals agreed on during the year] were terrible this year or whatever it could be – you need to know where people aren't happy. I don't feel bad if I call somebody and they're really unhappy and I can bring them to the company where they're going to feel appreciated and respected and feel like they're compensated correctly. I have no qualms about that. I don't believe that recruiters should attack one company and destroy that company. There are companies that do have that kind of attitude, we don't – I don't believe in that. I wouldn't stay with a group that believed in that.

There are some great books on data collection, recruiting, sourcing, finding stuff, and developing those skills. It takes a lot of time to play around. Shally Sterkel has some interesting things online. You can look online and find some great techniques to build on.

Marcia: Do you have some advice for candidates in general?

Noelle: I was on a panel this week and I asked, "How many people have been to an interview and never have gotten feedback?" Most of the hands went up. I said, "Well, did you call back?" And they go, "Well..." If you were looking for a sales job, that could have been part of the interview process. There was a recruiter that piped up and said, "We do that all the time at our company. We want to know how interested a person is to call back."

You're a part of this whole process. It could be that you fell through the cracks. I've heard people that called back and they say "We forgot about you!" That happens – it does. Or it was part of the interviewing technique: let's see if they call back. If they don't call back, how interested were they? You really owe it to yourself to call back and find out what's going on and say you are interested. Sometimes they (candidates) don't say they want the job in the interview or they don't ask, "Do you have concerns about my ability to do the job?" So just say, "Do I fit in?" or "How do you see me fitting in?" I think it's important to say in the interview process, "What are the problems here?" Then tell them how you can solve the problems with your experience and what you bring. If you don't have exactly all the different features and functions they need for that job, just say, "I'm a quick learner, I'm a quick study. Do you have concerns about my ability to do this job?" They will tell you. Ask them what they're not going to tell you.

I think that recruiters ought to tell candidates how to dress for that company – especially in the Silicon Valley. I had a guy call me here and I'd met him at a networking event a while ago. He's a very good candidate – project manager – and he said he interviewed here five times. I go, wait a second. Nobody should have five interviews with five different teams and not get hired. There's something wrong, because there's no way you should have to interview 5 times and not get hired unless you're working at 1 of our competitors, that it takes 10 interviews to get 1 hire. We don't work that way. So, I couldn't figure it out and I asked, "What did you wear?" He said he wore a black tie and black suit. I go, "You weren't going to a funeral! This wasn't an evening event." I said, "Do you know you only wear a black tie and black suit during the day if you're going to a funeral or evening event? You never wear a black suit during the day." He goes, "I never knew that." I said, "You don't. Does anybody else have a suit on here? No." And this was an engineer – he didn't realize what to wear.

10

Marcia: That's a good point, because in the Silicon Valley, people walk around in very casual clothing at some companies and some companies dress up a bit more.

Noelle: Well, at Company X, I heard that if you don't dress up, they're insulted even though they're all dressed casually. At Yahoo! unless you're going for a sales job – in a sales job you would dress as if you were going to a sales meeting – which would be your best clothes. You're wearing business casual for anything else. I had a friend interview here; I saw her in our parking lot and she had a T-shirt on and jeans and she got the job, not a problem. But I would say that was probably a little more casual. But, I would say wear khakis or very casual pants that you're comfortable in. People need to ask, "How do you dress for the interview," because people want to hire people like themselves. When in Rome, do as the Romans.

When you come in match the energy of the person interviewing you. If they're low energy, lower your energy, if they're higher in energy, raise your energy, and so on. That's why interviewing is exhausting.

Marcia: Do you have additional thoughts?

Noelle: Candidates sometimes expect somebody else to do a lot of the work for them. It's harder finding a job than doing a job because there's a lot more emotion that goes with it. You feel you're putting yourself out there and it can be a rejection. That's why candidates don't call back. The idea of reaching out and telling people that you need a job becomes like a phone phobia. If you're looking for a job and you're between jobs – and we all have been there – don't spend your whole day looking for a job. You'll get job burnout and you really won't be ready for a job if you get one. If I was between jobs, I'd have it on my answering machine: "This is Noelle, I'm not here right now, I'm out looking for my next recruiting gig." People don't always know you're looking for your next gig; it just helps your network.

Even when you have a job, you have to be out there networking and also giving back at the same time. You can't just say, OK, I'm good. There are people who have worked eight, nine years and I say, "People don't know you outside of your company. You need to be out there giving back, being on panels, talking about recruiting and networking for your next job." It's like people that don't go to the HRCA - you really should be going to those meetings and networking with the Silicon Valley Women in HR. Why not? You should be part of that. I know a lot of people who have had lasting relationships, friendships and business dealings, because of going to your group - Silicon Valley Women in Human Resources - so it's very important.

Career development is not somebody else's responsibility – it's your responsibility. Corporations are not your family. People think that the corporation is your mommy and your daddy but it's not. It's not a primary type relationship – in sociology – it's a secondary type relationship and it's a business. People who are conscientious and do a great job are going to have lots of opportunity, but your career development is your job – not the company's job. The company will have opportunities for you, but they're not going to tell you which one to take. You're going to have to seek those out and do that on your own.

Steve Watkins

Steve has been a database administrator, a search/research recruiter and is now in business development for Unitek, an IT Training & Consulting Services company in Fremont, CA. He has some wonderful stories about research and business decisions.

Marcia: How long have you been recruiting?

Steve: Since I got out of college in '92. My first employer out of college was a recruiting firm, which was accidental since my Bachelors of Science in Physics had very little to do with recruiting. I wanted to be a high school Physics teacher, but after graduating I realized that to teach anything besides elementary school I would likely need a Masters degree. And even then I would not make more money than I could make in the recruiting business. The accident happened this way: A few months after graduating with my Physics Degree I looked in the want ads of the local paper - do people still find jobs that way? -- and saw an ad that said: "Want to be a Headhunter? No experience necessary, technical degree preferred." I thought: I don't know what a "Headhunter" is but it sounds cool and I have a technical degree, so I'll apply and see what happens. So I sent a resume and got called for an interview with the owners of this executive search firm in San Francisco that specialized in biotech. After the interview they said "Well, you don't know anything about recruiting and you've never had a job doing heavy phone calling and you're not very aggressive" - implying that my social skills left something to be desired, which they did at the time - "But, you seem to know these computers pretty well. Why don't you be our Database Administrator?" So I was the Database Administrator for a year and a half, with all these people doing search/research and recruiting around me. I started to take on a little bit of their tasks, a bit of their detective work: calling for information, finding out about the companies we were targeting for recruitment and miscellaneous phone calls when they were shorthanded. By osmosis I learned the recruiting process and discovered I was good at the front-end research & profiling.

Marcia: Tell me what research and profiling are.

Steve: "Search/Research" is the starting point of most recruiting because you can't recruit people if you don't know who to call. Most recruiting projects start with the huge umbrella term of "research," which could mean research on target companies to go after, such as the competitors of my client. It also includes research on people, such as finding the people within these companies to call. The people-research tends to be called "search/research," which is a catchall phrase for every possible method of detective work to find the people doing the job I am recruiting for at a target company. Once I know that, I hand that information to a Recruiter or Profiler to further qualify that person and hopefully gain their interest in the position my recruiting firm is being paid to fill.

Marcia: Doing research and finding names is a lot easier now with the Internet. It wasn't so easy at that time. How did you find out who was in the organization?

Steve: It was generally by two methods. There were people who did massive amounts of networking, going to conferences, collecting business cards, calling people - who build a web of networks usually within a community of the same kinds of people. You'd have people that built networks in the semiconductor industry only, or they only dealt with salespeople because salespeople tend to know other salespeople. I didn't do that because, again, the bad social skills.

I did what most search/research people did, which was to work purely on the phone. If I have to find out who the manufacturing engineers were at the Intel plant in Phoenix, Arizona, I had to call and figure it out from various conversations and wrong numbers and voicemails and transfers. It's a shotgun approach calling initially; asking the right questions to get the right information so they point you in a narrower way towards your target. Eventually you're talking to someone who works there and hopefully, if you ask the right questions, they will tell you who else works there. But it's a lot of phone detective work - currently people call it "social engineering." If you Google social engineering you'll find a lot of methods employed in search/research.

Marcia: How did you keep track of all of these names?

Steve: Well, in my first job I was the Database Administrator, so officially my job was to keep track of the names! Keep in mind that in the early '90s there was no Microsoft Windows. People were using DOS-based databases like FoxPro and most small search firms at the time had their own contract database developer who would come in once a week and make updates and enhancements: are the reports running right, do you need a new search functionality, do you need any new fields? Everything was done in WordPerfect where I worked and Lotus spreadsheets were a common "contact database" for many recruiters who couldn't afford to develop their own custom database. I think the first time anyone in the recruiting world really started using a software application that was intended to sort and categorize people was when folks started using "Act!" contact management software. By the late 90's there were software companies making database applications specifically for the purpose of recruiting & staffing information storage.

At the time I knew recruiters who literally had the "master spreadsheet" that they've used forever and if they had to find someone they would sort by the name column; if they had to find a company they would sort by the company column. This could be a huge 20,000-record spreadsheet, so they would do their search, leave, make breakfast, come back and it would be done. I knew other recruiters who used a big word processor document. Literally they would do Control-F (Find) and would find their candidate information wherever they happened to have typed it in the document. It was a time of "use whatever tool you're comfortable with and fly by the seat of your pants."

Marcia: How long were you at the agency?

Steve: I was at the first agency about two and a half years. They started out tasking me with the easier phone duties, things like "We already know who this person is, we know what he does and it's a really easy job description - just call and see if he's interested." When they were shorthanded they tossed that work to me. Slowly the candidate contact work became a little more advanced and at the same time there was the research work. We were a biotech-focused company so I had to find large lists of potential candidates for common biotech & pharmaceutical job descriptions. Every week we were looking for a Director of Quality Assurance or a Clinical Research Associate. My job was to identify the professional associations that candidates belonged to and what conferences they go to. I would get a list of attendees, a membership list and who is speaking at these conferences. A lot of my job was to find sources of information in large quantities, put that into the database and then hand that to the recruiters as a *source* for candidates; hence the word "sourcing" as a synonym for "search/research."

The part I enjoy most is the upfront research part before you talk to anybody. I enjoy the detective work of weaving the web of phone calls to get to the right person and bouncing around the company and finally talking to whomever it is I need to meet. You get the lay of the land, such as what industry I am dealing with, who are the major players, what are the major events or places these people go and also researching the "one level up & one level down" information: Who are the coworkers of this kind of person? What job functions report to this person? What job function does this person report to? That preliminary information gathering gives you knowledge of what this job function does so you can better hold a conversation with someone. The worst thing you can do as a recruiter is have a conversation with someone who asks you a question you should know if you cared at all what they did for living. They expose you: "You don't know what I do, do you?" It makes them feel like they are just a warm body to you, and you don't really care about this. You should be able to hold a conversation with the kind of person you're trying to recruit as if you were an entry-level version of them. To me, that's the fun part of the research, because you learn the lingo of a new job, the ins and outs, the buzzwords, the acronyms and the crazy stories about how they do their job.

I enjoy candidate recruiting once I know who is to be recruited and if they are at a fairly high-level. Usually the staff-level people haven't been recruited much and you have to almost teach them this process. They don't want to talk to you and don't understand why you're calling. It's kind of painful to be the first recruiter someone's talking to because you really hold them by the hand. But if you call someone with 20 years in the industry, he's already been recruited 5 times in his life and had 500 recruiter conversations. He knows the drill and it's quick and easy.

If I'm talking to someone who I can tell doesn't know where this conversation is going and doesn't really understand why I'm calling, the easiest thing for me to do is say, "I'm working with John Smith, the manager of software applications at Company X. He asked me to help him find people who can do ABC for some development initiative" – I may or may not tell him what the initiative is – "I was referred to you as someone who gener-ally works in this field and although I don't know if you specifically do ABC, you probably know someone who does ABC. I want to find out if you can help me in this process to identify someone who has this particular skill set." Sometimes I find it helpful to be vague about specifics of money and job func-tion. Sometimes it is bad to say, "For a full-time salaried position that pays X, I'm looking for someone to work in this job role with this skill set." Some people like that exactness, but by being so specific you increase the chance that they will not qual-ify themselves by not being a bull's eye fit. Most people are more likely to continue talking to you if you only give as much information as they need and no more. The moment you give more information than is necessary, that's a reason for them not to continue talking to you. They may say, "Oh, that's below my salary range." Click. "I'm already a manager, I don't want a staff position." Click. "I don't want to move." Click. Even if that's true, you shouldn't lose the opportunity to have a good conversation with this person and leave them with the feeling they knew they weren't right for what I was looking for, but we had a nice conversation. If I am in the market for something that is in my line of work or my next career goal, I'm going to call that guy back. You want to have a conversation like: "I know you work in this industry, I work at companies who need people in this industry from time to time. Maybe you're not ready now, but *if* you were to make a career move, what would that move look like? What would cause you to leave, what amount of money or what work environment or what job would cause you to stop do-ing what you're doing now and go do something else? If I see that opportunity I will definitely let you know."

People are usually very willing to describe that dream to you and if they've described it to you, even if your job doesn't match their dream role you can say, "Well, I'm not recruiting for your dream role. I'm recruiting for this other thing that's not exactly what you want but sounds like you wouldn't want that." "Yeah, it sounds like I don't." "Do you know anyone who would?"

You want to get them on your side, by saying something like, "It's not that I'm calling to *sell* you something, it's not that if you're not exactly what I want I'm going to hang up on you. I just happen to be working for this one client company, and you happen to be working for that target company and I'm trying to find resources. If you're not interested now, that's fine, but we should keep in touch. At some point our paths are going to cross again."

Marcia: What did you do next?

Steve: I left to try recruiting on my own. I found I didn't have the discipline to work from home and ended up managing the search/research process for a company that sold candidate research and profiling services. One of that company's frequent customers was a contract recruiter who went from company to company and would use our services as the starting point to get his candidates. Eventually he landed at my current employer as head of staffing and realized he needed to have a full time search/research person working for him for his current company, as opposed to just using various vendors as needed for that service.

He, being a good recruiter, recruited me away from my search/research employer to go work for him in 1999 and I'm still at that company, although we are a very different company than we were then. I was recruited to do search/research and profile candidates for a team of about 30 contract recruiters we had placed at 30 different dotcom companies. All of these recruiters were looking for the exact same kind of people because they're at the exact same kind of companies. They all want Java engineers, web developers, an IT manager, a VP of sales, etc. Our company worked as a contract recruiting entity on one hand, but we also did placement of contract IT professionals on the other hand. My division supported the contract recruiting for our start-up customers who were hiring their own employees and this other division of our company supported our customers who needed contract IT staff.

Then the dotcom crash came and all that work went away. All the out-of-work IT folks decided they needed to get some more training to make themselves more marketable. Because my company had a small training division, it suddenly grew massively and since 2001 we've become a very large national training company that does a little bit of contract staffing and recruiting; a complete reversal from where we started.

I was one of about 30-something people and after the dotcom crash I became the one remaining member of that team trying to figure out what to do with the CEO of our company: we had this infrastructure and processes that lend themselves to staffing and recruiting, but there's no staffing and recruiting business. Do we close the business? Do we leverage our existing processes and infrastructure into some kind of work? We made a decision that the nursing shortage we heard so much about was something we might be able to solve because we are wonderful Silicon Valley expert recruiters and staffing people – surely we can recruit nurses!

We spent two years after the crash creating a Nurse Staffing division of our company, hiring salespeople and recruiters, building websites, making contacts in hospitals nationwide, doing daily candidate recruitment for nurses. We thought we were going to be the kings of nursing staffing.

We didn't place one nurse. Our company was trying to survive the dotcom crash and we sank two years of money into something we didn't make anything on. We learned a very important lesson in recruiting: in the tech industry we had been dealing with hiring managers who had virtually 100 percent control over their budget and their own hiring process. If the hiring manager in a tech company needs a Database Administrator and I say "I have a DBA and hiring him/her will cost you $20,000," then the manager would say "OK" and sign a contract and we would be done.

In healthcare I could have a conversation with the CEO of the hospital and say I have 14 nurses who are ready to go to work. She would tell me, "I don't have the authority to hire. You have to sign up as a vendor with our HR department." HR would say, "We have a full vendor list. We're not adding more vendors." I would say, "But you have nursing openings and I have nurses.

Your other vendors don't have these nurses. I do. Do you want them?" "Yes." "Are you going to pay me?" "No, you're not on the vendor list."

The paperwork and the slowness and the bureaucracy with which hospitals operated was mind-boggling. We had hospital HR staff calling us saying "I've found this resume of Nurse Jane Doe you faxed me five months ago – is she still available?" It became obvious to us that one reason there is a nursing shortage is that hospital staffing processes are so cumbersome. All our fancy IT systems, resume gathering systems, automated resume faxing and e-mail meant nothing – the speed with which we are used to doing this process in the tech industry meant nothing in healthcare – we were at a *disadvantage* because we didn't work as slowly as they did. So we closed that division.

We then had the same infrastructure, the same processes and the same problem. We wondered what we should do. By this time, our IT training division had been going well but we still had this staffing/consulting side of our company. We decided to focus on becoming a training company and keep recruiting and staffing as an augmenting service. If Charles Schwab sends 10 people to my Microsoft Systems Engineering class, that's great. I can call that IT Manager back and say "Hey, you sent your people to our training, do you need help staffing for any projects?"

From about 2003 or 2004 on, I've been pushing this staffing and consulting work because we don't want to leave money on the table from our training customers. It's an additional service but it's not the leading service. We don't get customers because we're a staffing company; we get customers because we're a training company. We tell them, "If you like the training we provided, we also have staff that can come work for you onsite." Because they've already had one good experience with us we'll maintain that relationship through our staffing work.

Marcia: Do you do any of the staffing now?

Steve: I do when it's recruiting people for our customers. We have a full-time recruiter for hiring our internal staff. She's wonderful; I only help her when we run into a brick wall and we can't seem to find the right people. I then kick in with the search/research and the sourcing functions. But when I need to place a consultant onsite with a customer I recruit the staff, do the paperwork, sign them and place them with the hiring manager – I do the whole thing.

Marcia: Can you picture staying in the field all your life?

Steve: Yes, because even though technically I'm not a recruiter right now, as a business function recruiting is the single most important thing to a company's success. You could have the best product vision in the world and if you can't find the people to implement it or make it happen, you have no product. I don't get paid to do recruiting - I get paid to send consultants to a customer or I get paid to create a training program for a client of mine. How do I find the trainers? How do I find the consultants? I know how to do that quickly from my recruiting experiences in the past. There is a line of training business at my current company and the reason we are the dominant player in that particular business is because we know how to recruit the people who deliver that business more quickly and more efficiently than our competition.

Marcia: If you were to give a candidate advice, what would you say?

Steve: There are basically two areas where candidates present information about themselves: a resume and the first phone conversation with a recruiter or a hiring manager. Overwhelmingly, it's the resume people are going to see first, just because of the way recruiting works. I have my mental list of things that people should never do, and these are mistakes that I see made mostly by junior people, but I've also seen executives make the same mistakes.

Some of the very common resume mistakes - their email address. I see a lot of resumes where the email address is clearly the personal address they've had since high school. It may have some kind of very unprofessional sexual reference or references their favorite car. I've seen so many emails like "hotstud69@yahoo.com" and it's on the guy's resume for a marketing position. What are you thinking? Get another email address! The less professional the email looks, the more unprofessional *you* look, no matter what the rest of the resume says. I also advise people not to put their hobbies and interests on their resume, because you never know when you're listing something that is something your potential boss hates. In my opinion, the less information about non-business things, the better.

A lot of people post their resume with a phone number. I call and they answer as if they're picking up the phone from a friend. They answer "Whazzup?" I hear a lot of people answering, "Whatup?" I say, "Is this, John, the guy who wants a position as an account executive?" "Yeah, that's me." Is that how you're going to answer the phone at my company? That first greeting should be exactly how you're going to talk at my company and if that's not how you talk on your phone, you'd better start. Talk that way for the duration of your job search. When you answer the phone it should just be "Hello, this is Steve." That first impression is amazingly important.

In the phone conversation, the worst thing is sometimes they talk too much. You ask: "It says on your resume you worked with Microsoft SQL Server 2000. Have you worked on the 2005 version?" That's a "yes" or "no" question. That's not three minutes of discussion about everything else that is related but not directly confirming the question. Then you have to say, "I can't tell if that's a yes or a no. Everything you've told me is interesting but I don't know if you answered my question." If you have some embellishment or interesting information, give that after you actually answer the question.

I've been on conference calls with the candidate and the hiring manager on the line and heard candidates interrupt the manager's questions and start speaking about something that's irrelevant. I've heard candidates not answer a question and talk about something else, rather than say, "I don't know." It's okay to say "I don't know" or "I've never done that," but if you're not answering the question, you sound deceptive.

Marcia: So be direct, honest and concise.

Steve: Exactly. It is not a bad thing to say, "I've never had hands-on experience in that," or, "I've read about it but I've never done it." Don't interrupt, answer the question and if you don't understand what they're asking, it's completely OK to ask "Could you explain that again." Because in reality you're interviewing them as much as they're interviewing you. This may be the guy who's going to control your paycheck for five years and you should ask some questions.

Marcia: Do you have advice for someone considering recruiting as a profession?

Steve: Figure out if you are the kind of person who is entrepreneurial and independent. If you are, it's a great profession to be in because you can work for almost any company anywhere if you're good at it. You can work as an independent contractor, as an employee; the types of employment are almost limitless. If you like a structured work environment where every day you do the same kind of thing, there are some recruitment jobs like that. If you're a people-person, if you are fearless about speaking to new people, if you display confidence in what you are saying; that is the difference between someone who is just following the recruitment processes from a manual and someone who can just hit the ground running in any situation. Figure out which of those extremes you fall into and realize there are staffing jobs for both and everything in between.

Once you understand your role and the goal of your job, and you can be completely confident in your ability to perform your job, that confidence over the phone with a candidate or employer sometimes counts more than the technical aspects of the job. I could be recruiting for the greatest job in the world for you, but if I call you and sound like "Oh, please take this job, I hope you really like it"; if I'm not too confident, it doesn't matter what the content of the job is. Conversely, I could be trying to fill the worst job in the world, but if I sound confident on the phone you will still have a conversation with me and I can still sell your information to the person who's buying it.

If you're considering recruiting, it's not enough to enjoy talking on the phone. That's not the core skill-set. The core skill-set is having complete confidence in talking to whoever picks up the other end of the line. It could be the CEO of the company or the Janitor. Can you change the way you speak to people, depending on what kind of person they are? If they're very methodical and professional sounding, can you speak very methodically and professionally? If they're very loose and casual can you speak loose and casual? Are you a good actor? I would suggest future recruiters assess if they are a good social actor.

2

CONTRACT RECRUITERS

Darlene Forsythe
Darlene has worked in third-party Human Resources
("HR"), at an agency, as an agency recruiter, Staffing
Manager, HR Specialist and HR Manager.

Darlene: My first job was with Kelly Services and from there I ended up working in third-party human resources. It's how I ended up getting into HR. I worked for a company on-site at IBM and it was the first time I thought, "I really want to get into recruiting in HR." I was working with the person who was the general manager in sales – director or something – and I ended up saying, "I really want to help out when we do roll-outs in finding people and getting the HR department set up." So I started doing that at IBM, and then they started letting me go out to HP and other clients they had. My job was to help out when we found people for interviews and start with training.

From there I went into, once again, being a third-party HR worker and was there for quite a while – I think three years. I started out as an on-site HR worker for Sun Microsystems, which was my first time really getting into the recruiting thing. We were onsite managing third-party vendors and we primarily tapped consultants for everything from manufacturing to accounting to other types, such as technical writers and administrators.

Marcia: When you talk about managing third-party, various vendors would come in with their temporary people for various positions, and you would coordinate contracts and times?

Darlene: We were the third-party resource working on site at a client's location and we did payroll services, so we had employees who were ours that were temps for, say, Sun Microsystems. The reason why I say Sun is because that's the one we started at. With the payroll services we managed, they were directly our employees. We would manage the third-party temps from vendors like Kelly Services or Manpower. We would help with managers who were directly with Sun, say, and would work with them around their requirements. We were the direct resource for the managers and we would work with the temporary vendors with requirements we needed. We'd get resumes, review them and get them to managers.

We managed the vendors who were getting the temps. It was interesting and fun. I learned a lot. After being there about a year, I basically became the regional manager for all the on-site workers. I managed anything from biotech, low tech, high tech, and all the people who were on site. I got to go travel when LSI had a new contract coming on board and help get it set up.

From there I actually did my only time working for an agency. I was the person who oversaw all the recruiters and that was the only time I ever did that.

Marcia: How long were you there?

Darlene: That one was a little less than a year. I decided I didn't love a lot of the things that went along with it and I also felt that I could do a lot better. The bad news was my old company wanted me back. The difficult part is after you're with a company for three years, it's hard when they say, "please come back, please come back", and since you're not as enthralled with where you're at you accept the old company's offer. I did that for a year -- I did recruiting, managed a staff of four recruiters, worked with the salespeople -- I did everything when you get a contractor on site. We were the people who were doing the back-end recruiting and we had salespeople that went out and got deals. I left and did implementation management for a year and decided it wasn't a good idea and I should not have run back.

Marcia: Tell me what implementation management is.

Darlene: I was the person who would set up a new account. I went in and got into the technical aspect of it. I learned how to create databases because that was one of the biggest things -- it was a solution so the managers were able to work with the system. We had to hire the staff, train the staff and get them up and running to work with the client contact directly, where they would figure out what their needs were for each particular site. Some of our clients needed more payroll services, which was one of our biggest things. They also wanted somebody to handle the temp or the 1099, and made sure they hired and had the right documents for bringing in 1099 contractors. That was what I did for a year.

After that I decided, I was ready to go in-house, which is what I did. I went in-house and worked for SiRF for five years. I started as a Staffing Manager and HR Specialist and after a year and a half to two years later I became the HR Manager. The nice part was I always saw HR from the outside until I worked at SiRF.

Dealing with a contingent workforce is a hard job because there're a lot of things that happen that may not happen when you are the person who's dealing directly with the workforce. You have a lot of intricacies with HR legalities that you don't deal with as the person who works as direct HR management.

Marcia: You're talking about employee relations, making sure that people have the right documentation, etcetera?

Darlene: Yes. Also understanding labor laws – you have to know them because you're keeping your client out of trouble, you have to know labor laws even more so, because you have a client who needs to know.

Marcia: How did you learn all these laws? It is intricate and involved.

Darlene: It is. The way I learned it was really taking upon them on myself. I had gotten involved with the NCHRA, so I took different classes through them. I also was one of those people who would take classes, I would go online, I would become friends with people who were within the HR world who were my clients. There was always at my disposal a way to find out something if I needed to know about it. I started that when I was the third-party resource and that's the reason why I left, because a lot of them didn't know about labor laws. That was my thing. I just said I have to find out. I would go and find out and go on the EDD website. I would go into anything that I could find and read up on it. Not everything I learned was from a class. I have my PHR and I hadn't gotten my SPHR and the reason why is I don't like taking tests.

Marcia: Having that network of professional acquaintances and friends, where you can ask questions is so valuable. How did you build that over the years?

Darlene: I have to say getting involved with the NCHRA was the best thing I ever did, because it was a place to go to really talk to people. I didn't have a broad range until I started doing that, because I think the opportunities were in front of me. I now know a lot of HR people and unfortunately we're terrible about networking and getting out there. We're all about socializing, not networking, and that's weird because they're two different things. One of them is 'How's your life?' and the other one is really making sure we know "What do you need?" How can you support each other? Sometimes we don't look at the fact there're a lot of things that people can do for each other. When you network, you never should be looking for your next job, by the way. That was one of the things that people needed to understand. When you network, it really is finding what does this person do, what do they need, what do they need from you, what kind of things can you help them with? I think that's the most critical piece about networking vs. socializing. I don't mean that in a bad way, but it really happens over a period of time.

You have to realize as an HR professional that broadening your experience to include people that will help you learn and grow is critical. Also, there might be some areas that you can help them grow in their business, or to help you grow your business or your professional life that is also critical.

Marcia: When you were taking the classes, and particularly the PHR class, how did you feel that that changed you as a recruiter? A lot of recruiters don't know anything about HR, and might even say illegal statements to candidates.

Darlene: Because I've always had the HR background with recruiting, I think that when I do talk to clients, the nice part is that I'm not the police. The nice part is that they know that I'm going to say the right things and then I'm also going to be able to help them. I also help candidates because people will say and/or do things they shouldn't do or say, especially when they've not done much interviewing, or they've come from a different country where the laws are very different. They may not understand how it works, or someone who hasn't interviewed for years suddenly wonders what the best way to do things is. Because of my knowledge, I think that it has helped in the long run for both my clients and for the candidates.

Marcia: If you were to recommend a career path and a good way to get into recruiting and HR for a new person, what would your advice be?

Darlene: I think that having a degree is a good thing, but I don't think it necessarily has to be in HR. I think having a really good business background is solid, because it gives you a good background. If you want to be in HR specifically, most companies are looking for someone who understands business, not just HR. Having a good business background is key, especially as we move forward in HR. It really comes down to getting the HR legal stuff because you do need that. Anyone who says it's easy just to pick up all of it – it's not.

When I talk to people now – the younger ones – more of them are getting directly into HR, but there aren't any young ones getting into recruiting and the contract recruiting in particular.

Marcia: They get there accidentally.

Darlene: Exactly. I think most people getting out of college are getting into HR, instead of getting into recruiting, which is interesting, because you can make a lot more money doing the other (recruiting). I think having a degree is important. Most people say, "Is that really important?" Yeah, I think it is –you're going to be able to have a higher salary just because you have it. If you want to do HR work there are some classes you've done or maybe that's your minor – that's great. If you want to be an HR Generalist, a lot more companies are looking for that, but if you're not sure then having a good business degree is a good thing. With a business degree and taking some classes through the NCHRA, or taking some classes with SHRM or taking some night classes can help. I did that so I think that's really great.

For somebody who maybe has already graduated and you want to get into it now, that's what you do. That's how you get the background. Do you have to have the certification? No. But I think once again more and more companies are requiring a certification if you want to be a generalist or a specialist. The nice part about being a recruiter is you don't. Really what it comes down to is: do you have the personality to do recruiting? Is it something that you'll really enjoy, because if you don't, then don't do it. The bottom line is there are a lot of HR people who will never like recruiting. If you like to talk to people and learning about the company you work with then you should get into recruiting.

Marcia: What makes a good recruiter?

Darlene: A good recruiter needs to be able to research their client company and understand their technology, because a recruiter needs to portray that knowledge to a candidate and to be able to talk to the hiring manager. If you don't, you're going to be like every other recruiter who can throw paper. Unfortunately, that's what hiring managers quite often think. If you want to impress, keep your job and be able to feel like part of the team, then know the technology of the company.

Marcia: Could you talk a little bit about the changes in technology over the years as far as recruiting is concerned? Both for reaching out to candidates, finding candidates and internally how you use technology to track candidates; how do you keep on top of all of that?

Darlene: Over the years, I think we've all used many different methods. Back in the day we faxed resumes, which was horrendous because it took hours to go through. We also did advertising in the Mercury News and Westech job fairs. At the Westech shows we would sit for a day or two and meet whoever we could and it was funny because we'd all see the same people. The nicest part about recruiting now is the Internet, because it makes recruiting quicker, better and faster. It's also nice because you have more choices to post your jobs.

The other part is that Hot Jobs, Monster, Dice, or whoever you're using, have become tracking mechanisms. If you're someone who doesn't have the money to get an applicant tracking system, you could use one of those websites. We all know if you're a public company who's doing government contract work, you have to do that. But the bottom line as a recruiter is you want to track because you want to remember why you liked this person or disliked them. You could use Excel and do that but that's the old way. I've never used Resumix but some of the bigger companies use Resumix. That's now become one of the older technologies of tracking resumes. Nowadays they have a bunch of different ones you can use for applicant tracking. I like the applicant tracking mechanisms, because you are able to track when you interviewed, what your feedback was and you can do e-mails directly from it. It's the best way to track what you're doing for future reference; because we all know having a database as a recruiter is the best thing to have. If you don't have a database with your candidates then you're always going out to find them, whether that's posting or sourcing. If you have a database of everyone you've ever talked to, that is gold.

Marcia: Could you talk a little bit too about what makes a good candidate for a job?

Darlene: What impresses me first is a resume and a cover letter. Some people say they don't like cover letters. To me, a cover letter gives me the idea that a candidate looked at the job and has a clear understanding why they are a fit. It really shows me that a candidate is interested.

A good candidate is someone who has a resume that's clearly a good fit for the job. In other words they have the technical skills, software skills and have actually spent the time to make sure they are a good fit.   Also, a resume should not be too long. If a candidate has more than a two- page resume they better have a good reason, because he/she should be able to figure out how to capture their skills and experience in two pages – maybe three if you've been around for 20 plus years. But if a resume is 4, 5, 6 and even 16 pages it's horrendous, because there's not a hiring manager around who wants to see it. [This is different for scientists or biotechnology employees. Their resumes or CVs tend to be very long.]

When I conduct an interview my expectation is that a candidate will at least know what the job is, who the company is and has done a little research before I talk with him or her because that shows interest in the job. When I talk to a candidate, I really like it when the person has relevant questions about something you haven't learned on the Internet or about the job itself.

The other thing I like about candidates is when they listen and answer questions I'm asking. I find a lot of times that someone will tell me what they *think* I want to hear, vs. what I'm asking.

So to me, a good candidate is someone who's really done their research. They should be prepared, be open with a recruiter and understand the recruiter is your friend, because they're your first way into a company. If you think they're the stopgap before getting to the hiring manager, unfortunately it can impair the interview process or even stop the interview process.

One of the things I have to say that I hear quite often is HR recruiters are not the doorway in but more like the doorway to stop. That's so not true, because my hiring managers count on me to give feedback however I have to tell you, if it's someone that I didn't have a good experience with, they're not going to bring them in. That's my biggest thing I have to just tell anybody.

Herb Deitz

Herb has been a teacher, in-house human resources generalist, recruiter, staffing manager and contract recruiter. He has had a wide variety of experiences in different industries and is passionate about recruiting. To provide full disclosure: he is my former husband.

Herb: I taught seventh grade world history in New Jersey and at the same time I was working retail at Two Guys Department Stores from Vornado ("Two Guys"). That's where I first got started in recruiting. I worked at Two Guys during the summers when I had time off from school and during the evenings while in school. I worked retail and eventually I began staffing entire stores. I had to staff an entire retail store, which was usually at least two hundred employees. Two Guys was both a food and non-food store so I had to hire a lot of people.

In my early years, I wanted to be a sports writer or a sports broadcaster and I thought, I'm going to have to interview athletes, so I ought to learn how to interview. I took some general courses on interviewing and that's where I first began recruiting at the retail level, which is really different from what I do now.

Marcia: What's different about retail? Were you also hiring into unions?

Herb: It was a very strange situation because I was part of the Retail Clerk's Union, but despite that, I was in management. I ended up hiring retail clerks but I also hired people that weren't going to be retail clerks. My hiring ranged from manager of departments to salespeople, to grocery clerks to people that would stock the shelves. When I staffed the store I started with a shell of a store and hired two hundred people. I got involved in a whole bunch of different types of hiring.

Marcia: How would you find the employees?

Herb: We'd run newspaper ads on occasion and radio ads. We would also do some billboard advertising, but it was very limited because I'm going all the way back to roughly 1976. I ended up moving from New Jersey to California and when I moved to California, I had gotten out of hiring entire stores and I was part of the camera department because I really got into photography. One of the individuals that I became friends with at the store was Michael Jarvitz, an engineer from New Jersey who worked for Data Products. Mike said to me, "Why don't you come down and apply at this company that I work at?"

Back then, Data Products was one of the leading manufacturers of large printers. I was so incredulous about going down there, because I didn't know a transistor from a resistor. I went down in my tennis shorts and I filled out the application and I thought, there's no way – there's no way. There wasn't anything for six months and then I got called by the Director of Order Administration and the Manager of Order Administration. They took me out to dinner and they liked me enough to offer me a job.

My very first job in technology was being an order administrator. There were three thousand parts to that printer and there was no computerized way to locate parts. We had a big book and I had to look through all the different parts. When people called we had to get them the right part, write the part down and then someone would keypunch it into a machine and then send the parts out for the printer. It was really stressful because when the printer went down, these companies could not run their business. It was mission critical that we had to get a part and we got it. But we had tons of telephone calls – maybe thirty to forty telephone calls a day. We got fifteen to twenty-five faxes a day from international folks that had our printers. We had to always keep the parts moving. And they wouldn't order one part; they'd order a whole bunch of parts.

To show you the difference in where we are today, one of the parts we had was a three thousand dollar part our customers would have to order. Without that part the printer couldn't run at all. So when I got one of those parts we had to get it out the next day. I did that for about six months and it was very stressful. And then I said, "I don't want to keep doing this the rest of my life." But it was fun being in technology.

Around 1978 I asked for a transfer into Human Resources and I got very fortunate. I ended up being the HR Generalist and anyone at Data Products – there were three thousand employees at the time – that wanted to transfer from one job to another had to come through me. I had my own secretary and I had to learn all the jobs at Data Products – the engineering jobs, the marketing jobs, the finance jobs. I had to read about all those jobs to get up to speed and understand what they were transferring from and what they were transferring into. I'd have to interview them and I had my own administrator. I did that for probably nine months.

Marcia: How was it that you asked to transfer into HR? Did you just figure that's a good match because of the work that you had done at Two Guys?

Herb: With retail, I was what they would call an operations manager, but a lot of it had to do with human resources: hiring, interviewing, benefits, talking about wages and things like that. I thought I'd like human resources and I'd be good at it. It was the best break that ever happened to me to have to learn all these different jobs. It was almost like a self-taught course on what positions are in high technology.

Marcia: Did you have anybody who would explain what some of these terms were, or did you muddle through that yourself?

Herb: It was a combination of muddling and certainly talking to some people. Some people were very nice and they took pity on me and said "This is what 'what you see is what you get' is." Some of the people did help me, but for the most part, it was a lot of muddling through.

I did that for about nine months and I really got up to speed on what a hardware engineer is, what a software engineer is and what a quality assurance engineer is. It was a great education – great - and I was getting paid for it. Then I decided, I've been here nine months and I want to do more recruiting. I want to do more staffing. I ended up moving to a company called AM Jacquard Systems.

AM Jacquard Systems was a company that used to be called Jacquard Systems until it was acquired by Addressograph-Multigraph – A.M. We grew that company from a hundred to about seven hundred. I had a great boss, Bob Pardue. Bob was really helpful because he loved doing policies, procedures and processes. He was great at that and hated recruiting, so he said, "It's all yours." It was my first real taste of recruiting because I was called an HR Manager. I did some employee relations and affirmative action but for the most part I did heavy-duty recruiting. When you're with a startup, you get everything thrown at you. You get everything from accounting and finance to sales and marketing and certainly engineering.

Marcia: What did you use to recruit that many positions?

Herb: It was mostly newspaper advertising and it was calling people up and asking them: "Who do you know? Who do you know? Who do you know?" It was joining associations like high tech associations or even Jewish associations and really trying to network, network, network. This was roughly about 1979 through 1981. I was there about two years and I probably hired about two hundred to two hundred and fifty people in that two-year time-frame.

A quick story is that the Director of Facilities got really angry with the company and got up and left. My boss, Bob Pardue, said, "You're in; you're the Acting Director of Facilities." So I had the mailroom, the receptionist area, security and some other areas. Now that was really hard because I had no idea what the mail room did or what security did, but it was interesting. I did that for about a month and boy, I did find a Director of Facilities real fast.

Marcia: There's your incentive! You don't find somebody; you're going to go do it!

Herb: Unfortunately, at Jacquard the product always did really well; it won awards, but the public just didn't buy it. We all could see the handwriting on the wall and I started to have to lay off people. I had to lay off all those two hundred and fifty people I hired. I ended up going to a company called Micom Systems. It was in Chatsworth and then it moved to Simi Valley.

I went there as an HR Generalist. I took a demotion and that was a big mistake because I learned the hard way that once you've been at a certain level, it's very hard to go back. But Micom was a company that was just growing incredibly. When I joined them they had roughly seven hundred and fifty employees and in three years we had grown to over three thousand. I moved from an HR Generalist to, you guessed it, Staffing Manager again. I ended up with seven people reporting to me. That was my first taste of managing a group and managing a staffing operation or staffing function. It was heavy-duty interviewing, recruiting, affirmative action, some training and development, but it was very good training for me. It really stood me well when I ended up going into business for myself many years later.

When the crash occurred in 2000, I was featured in a story in the New York Times. They asked, "What's it like to all of a sudden see the Valley crash?" It was really, really scary. I'll tell you – many, many people that I have a great deal of respect for that had been in the industry for a number of years could not find a job no matter what they did. I'm not just talking recruiters; I'm talking managers of sales and marketing and engineering – engineers with MIT degrees were out doing retail. They were out doing various other types of retail jobs where they were cashiers and clerks, because they could not find a job in the high tech field doing engineering, marketing or sales.

Marcia: When did that start to change?

Herb: I think that it started to change at around 2003 to 2004. Things started to rebound slowly. I ended up going to work for a company called VMware, which employed a hundred and seven people in 2000. By the time I left in 2004, we had seven hundred people. Today they're at twenty-five hundred people and they're close to a billion dollars in revenue. But that job enabled me to hold onto my house that I had bought. If it weren't for that job, I don't know. I think that by 2005, Silicon Valley became normal, if you could call Silicon Valley "normal." Since that time, I'd say it's been normal to high as far as the need for recruiting and staffing, especially in the area that I work.

Marcia: What is it that makes you a successful recruiter?

Herb: Number one, you have to really enjoy it. For some reason, I really enjoy the process after all these years. I started back in 1978 and I still enjoy what I do for a living. In fact, one of the big fears I have at 58 is what do you do when you're 65 or 62 and when you want to retire, how are you going to handle that? Because I really like what I do. You have to have the expertise, seasoning and experience of going through startups, going through working in corporations, going through working as a contract recruiter, going through retained search. There are so many different areas of recruitment that you have to have experience in. Because when you're on your own, you never know what type of client you're going to work for, or what type of situation you're walking into. You never know what tools in your toolbox of recruiting you're going to have to use in order to be successful with the client.

Marcia: You talked about the toolbox of recruiting, and I guess you could look on that as both skill sets and how do you keep track of data.

Herb: I think that the neat thing is it's almost like the Star Trek Enterprise. You go out and you never know what you're going to run into as far as new tools and new methodologies. Right now one of the best things that has happened to me as a recruiter is LinkedIn. LinkedIn has been incredibly helpful for me. When it first came on online, I stayed up until three o'clock in the morning looking at all the different names. That's how much I get into recruiting. There's another tool out there called Jigsaw, which is an excellent tool. There's also a new thing to keep your data straight called NimbleCat. NimbleCat is an algorithm-based product that will grade your resumes to the job description that you're looking for. If the resume matches the job description 80 percent, 70 percent, 90 percent, it'll tell you. And it's all algorithmic-based. If I could say it, I'd be a lot better off.

Of course the job boards are important. But the other thing – and unfortunately I would say from my days when I worked with Inktomi and when I worked at other companies that I've lost this a little bit – is pure networking; calling up people and finding out who they know. Because time and time again I have found your best candidates are people that are referred to you. The problem is everybody's looking for those people.

Nobody has time to talk to you and say you ought to call Jim Smith because they're looking for people or they don't have time. And you don't have time because you're busy attempting to reach as many people as you can to fill these various positions. The person to person, using the telephone to network is something that unfortunately has fallen out of favor with my toolbox. Unfortunately that's a very good tool when you have time to use it.

Marcia: Do you find that you're using e-mail?

Herb: Using e-mail is a great deal, especially broadcast email where you send out to a slew of people. When I look at recruiting, I think you've got to sit down and find out what does the client want? Not only what's on the job spec, but what do they really want besides the job spec? What are the intangibles they're looking for? What's the chemistry mix they're looking for? What's the cultural mix they're looking for? All those things are often completely disregarded by recruiters.

A second thing is a recruiter must have a battle strategy on how to find an individual. What are you going to do? Are you going to use Jigsaw, are you going to use LinkedIn, are you're going to use the job boards, are you going to network, are you going to put out broadcast e-mail? What are you going to do? What sets some recruiters apart is they know the tool they're going to use and the results they think they're going to get and more often than not they do get – that's your recruiter that's of high regard. If I use this, this and this, most likely I'm going to get this type of feedback or candidate input, then that's what people look for, because in the end, unlike a lot of areas of HR, with recruiting, you either fill the position or you don't. A lot of places in human resources, unfortunately, are soft. You may make a cultural improvement, or you may make a better-place-to-work improvement, or better training, but the problem is it's very difficult to measure that. With recruiting it's very easy. You either fill positions or you don't.

Marcia: It's filling them with low costs and in a prompt manner and with good candidates too.

Herb: Sure, and the other trick about recruiting is once an employee is on board, where a lot of companies miss the boat is retaining them; you want to keep them happy. One piece of advice I got was the VP of Engineering came up to me and said, "I don't want you to give away the store, but I want to make sure that every engineer you bring in is happy. Because if they're not happy within the first six months to nine months, if someone like Herb Deitz calls them, they're going to listen. And you know what? I don't want them to listen. I want them to be very happy working here. I want them to be challenged. I want them to be motivated. I want them to feel that they're learning. I want them to feel that they're making a difference. If they don't feel that, then I'm failing as an employer."

Marcia: Do you have some advice for a new recruiter?

Herb: Some people have innate personality characteristics that are helpful to being a recruiter. You have to have a curiosity about how to find someone or where to find someone, or what makes this person a good candidate, or what makes this person not a good candidate. So I think you have to have a curiosity, which has to be sort of innate.

40

You have to be someone who likes to be able to work in a non-structured environment. In many instances with recruiting, there's very little structure; you get a lead, you get a tip and you react to it.

You hear this over and over again – it's very overused and I hate to use it, but it's true – a recruiter has to be someone that's very comfortable with networking. It's just key. You can use the job boards, you can use the advertisements, you can use the post-ings -- and I do, despite being a very senior recruiter. I still use Craigslist and the job boards and I'd say maybe on a good year 10 to15 percent of my hires come from those pools. But the other 85% is from networking - from using LinkedIn and from asking who do you know. It's from dealing with other recruiters that know me and trading leads. Those are the things that someone has to be comfortable with and enjoy doing. If they're not comfortable with networking, or they don't enjoy doing it, then I just don't think they're going to be good at recruiting.

The innate personality, the innate intelligence, the innate curios-ity – if that is not there, you can't build that into someone. Having both the ability to network and to source and interview effectively, as well as having those other intangibles I men-tioned, are critical to be a good recruiter.

Marcia: Let me ask you about candidates. Do you have some candidates who were so stellar from the time you saw their re-sume or you spoke with them that just strike you? How would you advise somebody to be a great candidate?

Herb: Several of the candidates I met in '80 or '85 are now CEOs, or now run their own companies, or many of them have retired, or some of them have gone into the venture capital community. Unfortunately there have not been enough for me, but a few have. I'm working on a client now and they have this concept that they only want A+++ players, and we've heard that – you've heard that, I'm sure, many times. But what makes an A+++ player? It really depends on a few things. Number one, how professionally they handle themselves. Do they show poise? Do they also show the human aspect? Are they somebody you enjoy talking with? Is it someone that is engaging? Is it somebody that you find interesting? Is it someone that can teach you something you don't know? Is it someone who can impart with you in a down-to-earth manner what's going on out there in the industry and alert you to the things that you may not know or you may have a curiosity about? The types of people with those characteristics and a track record of success are the people that often are able to make it and do really well in technology.

There are several individuals that I've met throughout engineering, marketing, sales, finance and accounting going back 20 years, they had "it." They really exhibited that they were going to be players in technology and several of them have made it. There is always fate. There's always timing. There's being at the right place at the right time. It's knowing the right person. Those things also play a tremendous amount of influence on whether those candidates are going to make it all the way to the top.

Marcia: On the flip side, candidates that you'd rather not remember – you probably have some interesting stories of some candidates.

Herb: We don't have enough tape. There's a lot of that.

There was one individual that I'll never forget. I was a young, fairly good-looking-- I hope-- Human Resources Manager at AM Jacquard and a woman walked in wearing a very short skirt and she crossed her legs – something out of the movie Basic Instinct.

She handed me the resume and the application completely blank. I said, "I'm sorry, but you – you really have to fill out the application." She said, "You can take notes." I said, "All right, fine." I was taking notes and I said, "What are you looking for?" She said, "I'm looking for someplace – someplace to make my calls." Now, this is Los Angeles and I said, "Your calls?" She said, "Yeah, I do a lot of telephone work." I said, "Oh, so, are you – what are you looking for?" And she said, "Well, I think I'd be a very good receptionist." And I said, "Well, what's your experience?" And she said, "Well, I used to work an exclusive gentlemen's club, of which you would know nothing about." I said, "Well, I guess you're right." And that ended that interview and she did not get the job, thank goodness.

A second situation was there was a woman getting terminated and she was a secretary for an executive at this company. Again, this happened to be Jacquard and HR had to be with the person when they were terminated. So she comes out and her boyfriend, who happened to be Brady Keyes, a defensive back on the Pittsburgh Steelers in the late seventies, was waiting for her. I recognized him because I'm a sports fanatic. He looked at me and he said, "Are you responsible for this?" I said, "Well, not really." He says, "I asked you a question, didn't I?" I said, "Well, I'm in HR." He says, "Did you terminate her?" I said, "I had a hand in it." He said, "You did the right thing, son."

Marcia: You had a story when you were at SPC (Software Publishing Corporation): a woman came in for an interview with her top cut down to there – skirt cut up to there.

Herb: This woman comes in and she had the lowest cut blouse I've ever seen. It left nothing to imagination. She was very well endowed and she really wanted to get a job at SPC. I take her into a conference room and the conference room is closed off of course, but it can be looked into from the outside - there are windows that I'm facing and she's facing me, sort of. What I mean by 'sort of' is that she leans over on the table, and she dips and I mean, she dips all the way down. So there is no guessing about the blouse; it's all in front of me.

In order to have the desired effect, she also wiggled a little bit as I asked her, "So, how much recruiting have you done?" "Oh, I've done quite a bit," she said, shaking her shoulders. So, of course I'm trying my best to keep a straight face while everyone on the outside is laughing their toosh off– they know that I'm in big trouble. So, I try really hard to end the interview gracefully. I said "You know, I think you've got great qualifications, and, I'll be getting back to you," and she said, "Well, is there anything else I could do?" I said, "No, I think you've done quite enough." I said, "I think they're – I think we're fine now."

When I worked in retail I had just moved from New Jersey to Los Angeles. I worked at Two Guys and this woman came in with a live rabbit. I'm sitting there and I'm going, "Why would you bring a rabbit to an interview?" But I figured since I'm new in the area, maybe I don't know something. So she hands me the application and when I go to grab it, she said, "No, no, don't touch it on that side, the rabbit went on that side." I go, "The rabbit went on that side?" And she goes, "Yeah, he had an accident." I said, "All right." She was interviewing to be a waitress in the snack bar of the retail store. We're going through the interview and she's patting the rabbit all through the interview and at the end of the interview I said, "Look, I'm from New Jersey, I can't understand why you would bring a rabbit to an interview." She looked at me and she said – quite annoyed – "Look, can't you understand that it's better to have four good-luck charms instead of one?"

Marcia: Is there anything you'd like to add?

Herb: I think it's a great occupation. I think that too many people, including yours truly, stay in the corporate side too long. It's frightening to go out on your own, but I do think that once you've gotten the experience, once you've gotten the seasoning, once you've gotten to know how to network and you have a medium-sized network of people that know you and that you can contact – once you have those elements in hand, to stay working for a corporation is really counterproductive. You're no safer working for an organization or a corporation than you are when you're alone, in reality, especially in Silicon Valley. If this is true on the East Coast and Midwest, I'm not sure. But here in Silicon Valley you can lose your job due to a layoff, a takeover, or an acquisition just as easily as you could lose a gig when you have your own business.

You really have to have an idea in your mind of what you want to do when you go into your own business. You have to have an idea of how you're going to build the business, what type of tools you're going to need to carry out the business and how you're going to deal with your clients. One of the key elements to anyone's success in running their own business is repeat business, people that have worked with you and really value your guidance, your advice, and how you are to work with as an individual, or as your own company. That's what really sets aside many successful businesses, at least in relation to recruiting compared to the many businesses that don't make it.

Jenny Kahn

Jenny has worked as an in-house college recruiter and as a contract recruiter. Her love of recruiting, enthusiasm and humor are contagious. Jenny is the founder of a networking luncheon for recruiters in the East Bay in Northern California.

Jenny: I have been in recruitment for more years than I can remember. I started right out of college and I love it. I feel so blessed to be able to make a living doing what I love to do. When I reflect on it, it's something that I did my entire life, whether it was in a professional context or not.

Marcia: What did you study in college?

Jenny: I have a degree in marketing, which is a business degree – marketing with a minor in physical sciences.

Marcia: How did you get from marketing into recruiting?

Jenny: I didn't know recruiting existed. I graduated college and there was an ad in the newspaper for a tour guide for NASA and they were looking for somebody with a science major. My boyfriend's mother said, "Jenny, you should apply to that, you'd make a great tour guide!" I thought, well, they want somebody who has a bachelor's in science and I only have a minor in science, but she kept pestering me, "Jenny have you called NASA yet?" So I called NASA. The woman who picked up the phone said she could interview me tomorrow at two. I show up at two and I interview for that position and the hiring manager said, "You're not the perfect fit but we have another position you'd be ideal for, and it pays more. Would you be interested in a college recruitment position?" Pays more? Sign me up! I come back the next day and interviewed for the college recruiter position. Here I am, a new college grad and I got the job. Part of it was I had the right attitude and the right skill set. Part of it was the person doing that job was going to leave in two weeks and if they didn't fill it then, there would be no one to train that person, so they hired me.

Marcia: What attitude do you think it was that they saw in you?

Jenny: High energy, I think. A customer service, warm type of personality tends to fit this role. When I interviewed for that position, I said yeah, I can do that, sure, I'll do it. I was excited about it. I got to work at NASA. Stardust! Astronauts! Oo-oo-oo, yay!

I graduated in June and the next Fall I was recruiting students from my alma mater. It was interesting because I saw some of my classmates from other companies who were scientists or representing companies to try and pull alumni into their companies. It was interesting and fun, but if my boyfriend's mother hadn't kept badgering me to call NASA, if the recruiter hadn't asked me to come in and gave me no choice, if the person who interviewed me hadn't suggested me for that position, I never would have gotten it. I had absolutely nothing to do with getting that first job. I didn't even know the industry existed.

Marcia: How did they train you?

Jenny: There was minimal training and a lot of baptism by fire. There was a person who had done the job before who was there to mentor me. I was fortunate that I came in when the schedule was already set so I just needed to keep the train moving and on track; I didn't have to set the direction. My first job was looking at resumes and seeing who was appropriate to farm out to different places. I'd sit down with a stack that I had no clue about and I'd ask, "Rosalind, what about this one? Why would this one fit? Why wouldn't this one?" For six months I had those conversations with her once a week to go over the resumes that weren't obvious. After that I was able to do it on my own.

I joined an organization called the National Association of Colleges and Employers, which was a viable organization at that time but I don't know that it still is. They had events where employers would network with the career planning and placement people from universities where I would network and talk to other people who were doing career planning. I read a book on the subject and if you hang out with the people who do that and you're observant, you learn. I went from being the assistant manager of a college recruitment program the first year, to being the manager of the program the second year, with no supervision. I recreated the program in my third year and that was farmed out to some of the other NASA centers, which was kind of cool – I created some recruiter training.

Part of my job was to train the technical people who went out to represent NASA, on what to say and what not to say, how to represent the organization and to give them tools to be able to answer questions in areas that were not their expertise – such as, "No, I'm not in that area, but, let me see – yeah, we do that." I would give them tools to do that and the supplies they needed. I loved that job! It was like play. I would have done it if they didn't pay me.

I'm so blessed that I get paid to do what I do. My first two or three years there was just awesome and then I got to the point of "balancing the budget." They started to cut recruitment and as they cut recruitment, morale started to go and the organization went into this death spiral and it became a lot less fun.

I went from doing just college recruitment to also recruiting experienced-level scientists and engineers. That made it interesting for another year, maybe a year and a half. Then they weren't hiring those people any more and I had to go and be the cheerleader and advocate for funds to keep the pipeline going when they didn't want to pay for that, because they were looking at riffing [laying off] employees.

Marcia: We should backtrack to 'keep the pipeline going' - if they open up funds, or if people retire or change jobs for some reason, then you still have to have a flow of candidates.

Jenny: That's right and at this particular organization, it was very bi-modal. You had Apollo-aged scientists and engineers who had been there since the sixties who were waiting to retire to get their pension and young people who were straight out of college. There were not a lot of mid-career employees. We needed to keep that pipeline going and have that expertise within the organization. We needed to keep that knowledge on how to get those resumes out and what were appropriate resumes and keep the connections. A lot of it is public relations too.

I did all of that recruiting and then when the recruiting got even slower, I dealt with the foreign national visiting scientists with policy more than anything else including their work Visa paperwork. This was right after there was the spy scandal in Los Alamos and security was an issue and we began to wonder, "Who are these scientists that we are bringing over?" I got involved with the process that we need to go through for security, transfer of technology issues and what countries will we bring scientists from and what countries we do not. I went through, cleaned up and straightened out that process. Around that time I was fortunate enough to get a job outside of the government.

I went from NASA to Sun Microsystems during the boom and that was an experience. Sun Microsystems was one of the high riders during its golden time. The funny thing was, when I was trying to transition out – and I think this is really important and I tell everyone I talk to about this –when I wanted to make the transition from where I'd been for 10 years into a new area, I couldn't do it. I interviewed for two years and it was like I had "Government Employee" tattooed on my forehead and nobody would take a risk on me. The only reason I was able to get a job outside of the public sector was because I had networked and somebody championed me into the position. What was just amazing to me was before I worked for six months at Sun, I was getting called to be recruited out of where I was to recruit for other companies. What did I learn in six months that I didn't know before? But it's being at the right place at the right time and having perceived skill.

Marcia: How different was it for you in the work place, working for NASA versus working for a company like Sun?

Jenny: Here I was at a company that was like, "go, go, go! You've got an idea! Great!" Everybody was excited and happy to be there. At the time that I left NASA, it was getting kind of depressing and you could see the organization was in a down-hill spiral because the money dried up.

So it was a very different culture. It was also very competitive. I'd learned a lot about how important how you present yourself was and the power of influence: there were people who could get things done and people who other people liked to be around. There were some rules but rules could be broken if you knew somebody who was a real high flyer. You could see them and go boom, boom, boom, and be promoted in record time, where at NASA it's government, it's regulated. The Office of Personnel Management has rules about how you can promote and so to go from that regimented environment to, "Hey, what-ever goes, as long as it flies and it does what it needs to do, then go for it." You got great food and you got bagels on Wednesdays and come and wash your car and pick up dry cleaning and it was an amazing thing.

Marcia: Where else were you during the boom?

Jenny: I was at Matson, a semi-conductor capital equipment manufacturer. They make the machines that make the chips that go into wherever. They were a great company and probably one of my favorite places that I ever worked, because there was a wonderful group of people who cared about what they were doing. I was very successful there. I wasn't sure how success-ful I would be – you know, I had success at NASA, but that was maybe a fluke. At Sun I had sort of mixed success. I was really concerned about whether I was a good recruiter and what a good recruiter was. In that environment I was extremely successful. I hired a hundred people in five and a half months.

Marcia: What was your average requisition load?

Jenny: Never less than fifty.

Marcia: Were they different kinds of positions with different supervisors?

Jenny: No, a lot of them were duplicate positions. There were a lot of assemblers and technicians. There were onesie-twosies: I had to find a controller, I had to find a payroll specialist, I had to find buyer planners, but I was in charge of manufacturing. All of that manufacturing hiring I did with the help of a great team that had a great process. I told the manager, "I'll work as hard as you" and we kicked butt. I went from being six months behind to being fully complemented in six months. It was funny because the first day I got there, because they didn't have a recruiter for three months, I had five angry managers in my face, going, "Me first! Me first! I need resumes!" I'm like, "OK, talk to me about what you are, what you're looking for and this is how I work. You get back to me, I'll work with you. If you don't get back to me I'll work with somebody else who's going to move." But when I started I had 78 reqs. I said if I've got 78 reqs, I have lots to keep me busy and I'm not going to chase you.

Marcia: What tools were you using to find all of these people?

Jenny: We had the Internet and probably Monster, but I wouldn't swear to it. We used a lot of word of mouth. The assemblers knew each other, the technicians knew each other and they'd drag each other in. This was at a time when you still got paper resumes that would be sent in. We don't even accept them any more because you can't track them if they come by paper. People had sent in their resumes and they had no applicant tracking system, so we just had resumes in folders by the month that they had applied. So to go back and find somebody six months ago - it wasn't going to happen. Unless you had to find somebody for some sort of a reason, it wasn't going to happen.

Marcia: During the dot com bust recruiters all over were looking for jobs. What did you do to plan for that and how did you get by during that period?

Jenny: I was one of the lucky few that survived. And why did I survive? Networking. I can't stress it enough. My career has completely been made by networking. The first six months of the bust was really depressing and my mother-in-law said, "I guess you're going to have to do something else" and I'm like, "I love what I do!" How many people can say, "I *love* what I do?" I couldn't even imagine myself doing anything else. I kept networking and going to wherever recruiters gathered and I wound up getting a job doing outplacement, which is sort of the flip side of recruitment, because somebody at a networking event said, "DBM (Drake Beam Morin, an outplacement firm providing assistance to people how have been laid-off) is hiring and why don't you go talk to them?" The HR manager who got the resume used to work with my husband at the time so I was a known entity; luck played a lot in that. But I also would never have known that the lead was out there if I hadn't gone to the recruiter event.

I interviewed for that position and got a position training people how to write a resume, how to interview, how to negotiate an offer and how to network. In every class I was asked, "What career can I do where I won't get laid off?" I said, "What controls your career is not the industry you're in; it's your network and your network will tell you what's happening before it happens. It will give you the leads when you need them, it will give you the information you need to be successful. Your network will create your future."

Marcia: Speaking of networking, you created a group in the East Bay. Could you tell me a little bit about that?

Jenny: I had two really good examples to follow. My purpose in starting a networking group for HR people and recruiters in the area that I live was because I wanted to work for good people and I wanted to avoid the bad people. One of the ways you do that is you network with people and you hear their stories. I also wanted to work where I lived and you find those leads by networking with the people who work in that area. You know they say, "location, location, location." What comes out of my mouth is "network, network, network." You can't do enough of it. You have to have some life balance, but I have a hard time with that.

Marcia (the interviewer) had a networking group that I was a part of. That's how I got the lead into Sun, which really changed my entire life. I was so impressed with what that group did and how these women really helped each other and really made a difference in each other's lives and gave me friendship and a sense of community; it just gave me so much that I was grateful to be a part of it. I thought if I could copy that in some small way in my neighborhood, without having to go 25, 30 miles to get to another one then that would be a good thing. That's kind of what I based my East Bay Recruiters Lunch on. There was also one for the South Bay – it's a little different. It's got a kind of slightly different mentality but it was the same idea; that we get together for lunch and we talk and we shmooze and we talk about leads and find out who's looking, and who's got a lead. We just work together to support each other.

Marcia: Now you're doing contract work, and as a contractor your life is really different than when you're an employee. You have to market yourself, and that's part of networking, right?

Jenny: Being a contractor, you always have to prove your worth, because you can be gone any day. Because you can be gone any day whether it's your doing or not, so you need to have that network so that when you need to transition, you're not starting from Ground Zero. You know people and people know you. When I did my outplacement training classes it wasn't what you know or who you know, it was who knows you. So that when they're doing that cooler talk and saying, "we gotta hire somebody," they go, "Jenny's available." Or I could say, "Hey, I'm available, do you know anything?", and since I've already built that relationship they're willing to go to bat for me.

That only happens over time and through those networks. I kick butt in this job and I'm going to eventually be out of a job here and looking for the next position, so what I want to do now is start networking so that I can find the next position. I don't know who's going to provide me that lead, but I want to make sure that I've got a network of people who can help me do that.

Marcia: If you were to talk with a person who's considering being a recruiter, what qualities would you look for in that person?

Jenny: There are different kinds of recruiters and people go about recruiting in different ways. I think it depends on where you're at. If you're trying to hire an agency recruiter, you're looking for someone who's really hungry, who's really aggressive, who's going to go out there and pound the pavement and run, run, run! Greed is a good quality in an agency recruiter.

If you're looking for somebody who's going to stay the course, that's more of an in-house person; my bias is that you want someone who exudes warmth, who is an emissary for the company. You want someone who is intelligent enough to be able to understand what the company does, to be able to explain it to someone else, to be able to read a resume and understand what it is they're looking for, be able to see whether that fits somewhere else. A really good recruiter has the ability to see beyond words and understand the skills and apply that to a position that they didn't apply to. Like the woman who brought me into recruiting; I was applying for a tour guide and she saw the skills and said, "How about recruiting?" It is important to see transferable skills. To be an in-house recruiter you need to have a team spirit and some customer service sensitivity, because you may not want the candidate that comes in but you may want their best friend. If they have a bad taste about the company you're never going to get their best friend - you're not even going to get to see the best friend's resume.

Marcia: Do you have advice for new recruiters?

Jenny: Network, network, network! Find a mentor! The other thing that I really learned in my career was the value of having a mentor. It is huge, huge, huge. You save yourself so much grief and you've got somebody who can give you feedback, who can cheerlead for you, give you some sense of, "Look at it this way, Jenny," and "Maybe this isn't such a good idea." And sometimes just by example what they do is really important.

I'll never forget when you said, "Put away half of everything you make, because you never know when there's going to be a downturn." This was said to me during the boom when people were living the high life, mortgaged up to their eyeballs, drinking six dollar lattes and I thought, "Marcia says I need to do this, I'm going to do this." It was a really good thing because you had been around long enough to say it could turn and it could turn ugly for a while. I don't think any of us thought that it would downturn for six years. If I hadn't listened my life would have been a lot harder.

Marcia: Do you have some advice for candidates?

Jenny: You need to own the process if you're a candidate. If you're interested in the company, do a little homework: know who that company is and why you're applying to them. Don't be shy. Follow up. If somebody takes the time to call up and say, "I sent in my resume, did you look at it?" I look every time; I stop what I'm doing and look at the resume. That doesn't mean they're going to go anywhere, but I will give them the courtesy of looking at it.

I go to career fairs and people will say, "Look here's my resume and if you see anything that you think is a fit for me..." But that's not my job. If I see it and I think about it at the moment I've got it in my hand, you're lucky. I'm not going to remember you from the next person unless I make a real connection and you know what you're doing and I feel that you're a real asset to the company and I need to remember this one. You need to be responsible for looking at the positions and understanding what they are and whether you're a fit. Don't expect me to see that you're a fit, because right behind you is somebody who's done the work and they're the one who's going to get the job.

Good recruiters are wonderful resources - pick a few as friends. There's always somebody who needs a resume looked at or a connection made and recruiters by nature tend to be social creatures. They tend to understand the importance of networking and often can put you in touch with other people. I think a good recruiter is willing to do that.

Realize that not all recruiters are the same. There's a difference between an in-house recruiter, an agency recruiter, a retained recruiter and a contingency recruiter. It's important not to think that we're all going to treat you the same way. It's sometimes difficult to get into this industry, but it's a great industry to be in and I can't imagine doing anything else. You just need to knock on enough doors and make enough friends.

You can learn a lot if you go into an agency position. You're going to learn a lot very quickly, but it's going to be paid for. If you get an in-house position, you're probably going to learn – it'll be significantly less painful, but you won't learn as much as quickly. I'd rather take my time, which is why I've never been an agency recruiter. But there are different types of recruiters and different people see their role as a recruiter differently. If you want to get into recruiting, find a mentor who does recruiting the way you want to do it. Sometimes you learn just from observation, sometimes if you're lucky, you can say, "Can I ask you questions?"

J oe Compton

Joe has been in the military and has worked at retained and contingency search firms. The bulk of his career has been spent working as a contract recruiter, primarily in storage technology in the Silicon Valley. He's a long time active member of the HRCA and other professional groups and is a systematic networker.

Joe: I've been in recruiting for about 20 to 21 years. I ended up in the military out of high school and got a degree from the Naval Academy in General Engineering and spent 5 years in the Marine Corps. While I was in the Marine Corps all the people reporting to me had been drafted during Vietnam and since Vietnam was over they didn't want to be in the Marine Corps, and they didn't respond to all the leadership training that I had been given. So I started taking classes on motivating people and ended up with a Masters in Human Resources.

After leaving the military I went into sales and after about five years I went into recruiting, which in some ways convinced me it's an extension of sales if you're in contingency recruiting.

Marcia: How did you pick a degree in Human Resources?

Joe: It kind of picked me. I started taking these classes to help me on the job. Part of the job was, how do I motivate some Private First Class who is in the Marine Corps and doesn't want to be in the Marine Corps? Half the platoon was either in the brig, going up for court martial, or getting bad conduct discharges. My predecessor had been relieved of command because they had failed all the inspections. I didn't want to be next in line for that. I figured I better get this place functional fast. I was trying to figure out things that I hadn't been taught such as interventions to get them productive.

After I finished about four classes they said, "You take another six or seven classes and we will give you a Masters degree." So I said well what the heck. There weren't any wars going on, there wasn't a whole lot to do at Parris Island, South Carolina.

Marcia: What kinds of courses did you enjoy the most?

Joe: Organizational development. It's not like you're going to go in the Marines and talk to the generals about how you're going to change their organization. Their organization is set. But the case studies of the different companies, such as GE, I thought were very interesting. We looked at problems they had and ways to change an organization to make it better and solve problems.

Marcia: What kind of sales did you do?

Joe: First I was selling electronic components in Silicon Valley. That was one of the great no-brainers of all time in the early '80s. The company I was with was based out of Wisconsin and they sold the division I was with and laid everybody off.

I went to work with a computer equipment company when they had IBM mainframes, the tape reels and stuff like that. They were in the business to sell items for computer rooms, storage; not disk drive-type storage, but storage for tape racks and all the old IBM punch card drawers. That was an extremely dysfunctional company. Whenever I tried to get a hold of someone at the VP level, they were always seeing the company shrink. The directors wanted to be VPs, so they could go to the shrink.

I wanted to leave, I was looking for a job and I went to a headhunter, who had also graduated from the Naval Academy and he said, "Have we got a job for you." That's how I ended up in recruiting

Marcia: What kind of recruiting were you doing?

Joe: The parent organization's motto was that if you're going to be an engineering recruiter you have to be an engineer. If you're going to be a finance recruiter, you have to grow up as a finance guy, etcetera. That makes sense if you're talking to the candidates and hiring managers, but that's where the good part of the model ended. I still look back on it as a body shop. You're not dedicated to really helping the candidate, because they're not paying you any money. You're not really dedicated to helping with the employer, because you're just trying to find people that fit. I didn't like it for that reason and also didn't like it because there were no long-term relationships.

Marcia: Were you given any training or were you told: here's your desk, here's your phone?

Joe: There was training on how to close candidates - almost all on the candidates' side of how to control and close candidates. (How to manage candidates during the process until they are hired.)

57

Marcia: What would be an example of how to close a candidate?

Joe: Parts of what I learned were very good and I still utilize these practices today. Closing a candidate starts when you first talk with them. You ask them, "Why do you want to leave your present company? What is it that you're looking for?" You ask them all the other things like what their commute is, salary, bonus, how many stock options and when are they vested. You ask these questions so there are no surprises in the end. You still get surprised but you can't see it coming. But their idea was, "I'm leaving my company because they are not helping me with my career, I'm not being mentored." Well, great. So you show them this company. We had this manager that was known throughout the company as a mentor. He may have never even talked to the manager. You give feedback to the candidate based on what he's told you he wants and you give him the information that's important to him. Anything you can sell against the negative of your present company, changes to a positive with this company. You do some of that, but on a factual basis. My clients are what they are and they're not what they're not. If it's not a fit it's better for the candidate to go some place else that's a better fit. In fact, that's what got me out of contingency work.

There was a guy who was on an H-1 visa tied to his present company and they were treating him like a slave. He was way underpaid and in talking with him, the contributions he made to the company were phenomenal and happened to be in this industry. I talked with him and got him an offer with one of my clients and actually I felt really good about that. I felt like I could make a difference in this guy's life. He's going to get paid for a fair job. So he says, "I got an offer from your company and I appreciate that. I got an offer from another company." He was still on an H-1 visa and so he needed to be parked someplace for three or four years to get a permanent residency and I looked him in the eye knowing that it could feed my family, but I told him to take the other job. I think I resigned two weeks later. I wasn't cut out for that business.

Marcia: When you work at an agency, do you have a territory you are given and certain companies you can call? Or are you just told to call whomever you can to earn business?

Joe: I'll use the expression free for all. If you are already working with IBM or Intel, I'm not supposed to horn in on you, but you share the job orders with everyone else. In the company I worked with you're responsible for both candidate development and client development. You got no pay for client development. In other words, if I fill your job order, you got nothing for it. That was where the manager had to go beat on people to do client development.

I had a very low base salary and medical benefits, but I was commissioned and my salary was against commission. In a bad month where I got no commission I still got about $2K in salary and if I had a good month I made up for some previous months where I wasn't covering the base.

Marcia: The agency gets maybe 20 percent of the candidates' base salary; is that right?

Joe: We never did anything less than 20 percent. We might've had a couple of times when we had 25 percent, but mostly 20 percent. At least that's what the agency got. They provided phones, secretaries, Xerox machines and this was pretty much pre-computer days, so we had a large secretarial staff, which meant they re-write resumes from scratch. There was an overhead so a fairly senior guy was making maybe $60,000 a year - that was a senior engineer, so if you got 20 percent, it was $12,000. That number sticks in my mind; it was a very popular number. $10,000 to $12,000 was kind of the fee and I think we got maybe 40 percent of that, which was maybe, 35 to 40 percent.

Marcia: You went from an agency to... where?

Joe: I'd heard about retained search and I said there has got to be a different way of going about recruiting, so I went to a retained search firm. I went there probably more out of curiosity, of how they did it rather than thinking that was going to be my next career. I live in the East Bay and they were in Walnut Creek. Right after I started with them, they announced they were going to move to San Francisco. So I wound up working three months in Walnut Creek with them. I tried to commute to San Francisco for three months but I learned what I wanted to learn. It's very powerful the way retained search does their business and I've taken that model in-house for companies.

Marcia: In retained search you're searching for executives at a high level and the corporation pays a certain amount of money in increments as guaranteed pay to the agency.

Joe: Using round numbers, for a $100,000 position an agency will probably receive 30 percent or more. The agency would be paid typically 10 percent when they start the search and, having been in-house, there are a lot of reasons they do that because they're going to be spending a lot of upfront money and man-power to find some things. They receive another 10 percent when they produce three or four candidates that meet certain specifications and the final 10 percent is paid when the actual hire is made.

Marcia: What was it about their business model that you took into future positions?

Joe: The front end of the process is what the client is looking for. If they're going to spend all this time and energy developing candidates but the candidates don't meet the specifications, they've done all this work for nothing. There are a lot of times when your client doesn't really know what they're looking for and they're consciously or unconsciously using you as the recruiter to help them benchmark what they want in hard and soft skills.

When they deliver four candidates that meet the specifications, education, experience and all these other things and these guys are right, you better come up with a good reason why they are wrong, or you've just spent 20 percent of the salary of this per-son, and considering that this search is going to start all over from scratch for another 50 percent, which is fair, actually.

For instance, in an order for VP of Operations, once they've agreed with the client company and literally signed off on the job specifications, they'll research companies that would be like this company. For instance, if some of the operations are offshore, they'll look for companies that are probably based in the U.S. but do offshore manufacturing and are of a certain size, probably between $1 to 3 billion. They might also look at certain industries and make a list of companies. The next step is to identify who their VP of Operations is, or their Deputy VP or Senior Director of Operations, because it may be that person is ready to move to the next level.

For higher level positions, such as the VP, it's pretty simple to find that person. Today you can go to a website and there's Joe Smith, and he's the VP of Operations at a company. It wasn't as easy then and finding the Director today isn't easy either. You can do some research and go to another company and ask, "We'd like to know who reports to Joe Smith at this company." They'll charge 50 or 75 bucks a name, come back 2 weeks later and they basically say here are his 3 direct reports and their approximate job titles and off you go. Then it's dialing for dollars.

They take it from the name generation group and pass it over to a mid-level recruiter who's going to call that person and try and get a paragraph of information about them, which is probably not even revealing to what this particular job is.

> "I've got a BS from this school and an MBA from that school, I've been working 10 years ..."

> "If we have an opportunity, would you like to hear about it? Yes. Great."

Now you have 20 companies, 5 people per company and 50 people. You take it to a senior recruiter and two weeks have elapsed, maybe three. You call 10 people, you get 4 people who are interested; it's very powerful.

That's the model I took into a company that was in an explosive growth mode. I became the Staffing Manager and had eight or nine recruiters, hired a couple of sourcers, but there are always these reqs that are the impossible to fill; ones that bog people down and it takes so much time and energy to fill those that you ignore your other clients. I have a sourcer that works for me who is a fairly senior person, doing work for me at the junior recruiter level. I played the senior recruiter level in the model we talked about. We work on about four or five jobs at one time and after about four or five weeks we hired one person every week. As soon as we knocked one out I find another tough-to-fill job. Most of these positions were not at the VP level. In fact, none were VP level; they were all Director and below, which are hard-to-fill jobs.

Marcia: Back to retain search, what was your role?

Joe: What they told me was kind of interesting. You have to swallow hard when you're 35 years old and they say we're going to start you out as a researcher, because if the researchers are going to report to you, you have to understand what they do.

I did that for two weeks then I moved into what I'll call the junior recruiter role. I did that for a couple weeks until I took on the senior recruiter role and ran that whole department. The Principal, the owner of the company, would go out and interface with clients, bring back the job, specifications and benchmark, then come up with a list of companies. Sometimes she'd bring in a list of companies and we'd add to it and go back to the client and maybe cross them out since it was a subsidiary or they know the people at that company. So we get an approved list of companies before we make the first phone call.

Marcia: In the senior recruiter role, did you meet with candidates yourself or would that go to the other person?

Joe: Usually, the Principal met with them. I would develop the candidate to a certain level. Not all of them were at the VP or President level. There were some positions that a good client said, "We need a senior engineer." Sometimes we did the same exact program and come up with four senior engineers and the Principal didn't meet with those engineers.

Marcia: How are you paid when you work in retained search?

Joe: We received salary plus a quarterly bonus, as I recall. The bonus wasn't tied to any specific search and either you did a good job or you didn't do a good job.

Marcia: What are the qualifications to go into retained search?

Joe: That's a good question. I didn't do the hiring and that's another reason why I left the company, because they had about a 200 percent turnover. They would hire new college graduates and for the same reason they would put me on a research job for two weeks, they hire a new college grad and start them out as a receptionist. They were not telling them that they were going to start out as a receptionist. Why would you have a college graduate started out as a receptionist? I would think that name generation is an entry level career for most people. We had a middle-aged lady who had done that for 15 years and she was awesome at it. She trained everybody, including me and I think she's probably still doing that today.

I heard there were two other modes of recruiting: one being an in-house recruiter - an employee of a company; the other was contract recruiting. Contract recruiting sounded more interesting because, rather than going to work for a company for 10 years and recruiting the same thing day after day, I could go to work for a company for 3 months, 3 weeks, 3 years, whatever, and when I get bored with that skill set, I could move on. Very honestly, my wife works, she gets benefits.

Marcia: When you contract, you pay for your own vacation; you have no benefits, no sick time.

Joe: One of the clients I had in contingency search called and asked if I'd talk with him about some other jobs. That was my first contract, part-time.

Marcia: When you're working as a contractor, you are usually paid at an hourly rate. Have you worked on a contract where you're paid hourly and bonus or hourly and stock option or some combination?

Joe: Hourly and bonus yes.

Marcia: What is the bonus based on?

Joe: It happened twice. The first time was when I hired a candidate that was not an employee referral. Anyone I sourced, whether it was a person off of a Monster Board or I went out and said "who do you know"; however I found this person it was an external hire other than an employee referral and I would get - I think it was a $1000 bonus.

Marcia: How do you determine your hourly rate?

Joe: Two or three ways. One is very honestly, what is the market? I mean in 2000, if you could spell, "recruiter", you could probably get at least 70 bucks an hour.

What do you bring to a particular industry, if you have a wealth of experience as I do in storage? I have e-mail addresses in my Yahoo! address books - I say plural because I have four Yahoo! addresses because the address books get filled up with probably 800 to a thousand disc drive people. I also have three Rolodexes as I'm an old-fashioned guy. I go play golf with disc drive people. I go out to dinner with disc drive people. I go to weddings and funerals for disc drive people. My friends are in that industry.

Marcia: So that's who you network with and that's how you find new contracts too? It's through your network?

Joe: As it has turned out it has always been through my network for the last 14 years.

Marcia: As part of developing your network, do you go out to lunch, do you initiate invitations or how does that work?

Joe: This is my favorite subject. When I started contracting I was working for a company part-time and looking for something else and all of a sudden I found myself without a contract and out of work; now I'm scrambling trying to find another contract – well, there's something wrong with this model. The business model is I'm working so hard I don't have time to go find a contract. You've got to break that ugly cycle.

When I got a job in early 1994, I vowed that I would spend a minimum of 2 hours per week, 52 weeks a year, networking. If you're going to be a professional recruiter – well, there are professionals: there are teachers, lawyers, doctors that have to have certification and retraining each year. I looked at all these other things and thought, "What am I doing? I also vowed that on an annual basis I would take seminars and college classes to keep improving my skills and learn new stuff as it comes up, because technology was coming into play. Through networking I joined the Human Resources Consultants Association [HRCA], which was excellent and still is, by the way. I also joined NCHRA [Northern California Human Resources Association], which I've been less active in. The lunches, dinners, golf – if it's not with somebody from the disc drive industry, it's somebody from HR or another recruiter. That's why I have Rolodexes and e-mail files and all kinds of stuff. I don't have a database.

Marcia: How do you keep track of people - without that database and computer-search?

Joe: Let's say it's Friday morning – I'd go to the Rolodex and start at A and make three or four phone calls and put a little mark in where I last called and go to HRCA meetings, so that I make sure that I'm going outbound, if you will. The next week I'd start where I left off and it might take six months or a year to get through a Rolodex, but who cares? You receive an e-mail from me probably about once a quarter with some goofy joke on it, you know I'm still alive – I'm out there – it gives me a chance to say, "Hey, how you doin'? Where are you?" I wish I could send a Christmas card – a personalized e-mail to everybody – but I just can't. At least it's staying in touch.

Marcia: You mentioned the classes you've taken. Where do you go and what kind of class do you feel has been valuable for you?

Joe: They come under a couple of headings, like San Jose State has a whole family of classes where you can get a certificate in HR. I took their course on strategic staffing and there was another course I took before that – general HR type stuff. Knowledge never hurts. You go inside a company, even as a contractor and the employees there and the prospective employees look at you as HR. I had a contract at one company for six years and nobody knew I was a contractor. I looked and acted like an employee. They come to you with a problem so you hire somebody. Who's the first person that they're going to come to if they've got a problem, if they can't talk to their manager? They're not going to go to the HR Manager, they're going to go to the recruiter.

Marcia: That's where it's helpful to know what are really serious employee relations issues versus somebody letting off a little steam.

Joe: Right, and I'm not going to get involved with serious employee relations issues. You listen, you convince them that this HR person is really the best person to talk to, here's why. Sometimes you're just pointing traffic – here's the benefits person's name, call me back if they're not available or if you don't get the right answer. I go to a legal update each year on employment law, which had been through the Tri-Valley Human Resources Association out in the East Bay; a legal guy gives that presentation. The HRCA brings in top people, benefits people and people with new HRIS systems. It's another way of keeping current. You get business cards and become a resource for an organization. Somebody may ask, "We're having a problem with this, do you know anybody?" Well, the small Rolodex is nothing but HR contacts for things like that.

Marcia: In a recruiting position you have to keep track of technologies at companies to manage recruiting, and you have to keep up with the technologies at the companies that you're working with when you're talking to engineers so you under-stand are they qualified for this role or not. How do you keep up with all that?

Joe: Although I've spent a lot of times in storage, I have gone outside that industry for some contracts and it's amazing – I get the same question from people who prospectively hire me. My answer is that my mail – M-A-I-L – changes when I take a new job. Rather than getting Storage Weekly, I get Telecomm Weekly or whatever. You have to stay up on technology. You're not going to understand everything you read, but you're going to understand *nothing* unless you immerse yourself in that technology. The longer you're in it, the better of a resource you are to the company, the engineering management, line man-agement, etc. With the Internet it's very easy. You start looking up all these acronyms: they've got Wikipedia and all these things that you can get quick answers to some very basic ques-tions and you go to a manager and spend 10 minutes and ask, "Tell me about this." They're willing to teach you to an extent, and they don't want to take you from first grade to graduate level, but if you have the basics, they'll spend 5 or 10 minutes with you talking about the technology so you can do your job well.

Marcia: When you're at a larger company you have more re-sources than when you're at a startup. Where, at the start-up, you might do almost everything yourself.

Joe: I have worked for four multi-billion dollar companies. Only one of them had an applicant tracking system.

Marcia: Do you have other resources, such as sourcers?

Joe: I've only had sourcers at one company I've ever worked with. And these multi-billion dollar companies – two of them I was my own admin.

Marcia: At these companies you might be typing up part of the requisition or job description and going through the entire re-cruiting cycle?

Joe: The only thing I have different today from 1988 is I have a fax machine, voice mail and a computer.

Marcia: Of those technologies – which is the one that's most helpful to you?

Joe: Oh, I would say the computer because it gives me e-mail plus access to a lot of free job boards. With a computer you can find candidates and communicate, which I think is the most important thing. But you know that fax machine, still pops off about three times a day with applications. It doesn't have too many resumes, but it helps me communicate with candidates.

Marcia: You said something key a moment ago, which I find seems to be a thread – communication. You've got communication with the candidates within your own company, with the hiring managers, with the HR department.

Joe: That's key. I've been in some companies where there's a younger recruiter that sits in a cube sending e-mail to candidates and hiring managers and rarely are they ever on the phone. Going back to what I said when we started – when we're interviewing candidates and trying to find out why they're leaving their company, how can you close a candidate if you don't know this person? How are they going to tell you problems if you're faceless? They're not going to tell you what their issues are. If you know the issue, you have the chance of overcoming it. If you don't know what the issue is you're just throwing darts. It might be a money issue, but you don't know. But the standard thing is, "let's offer them more."

We had a candidate who was just finishing his PhD. His wife just got a post-doc in Washington D.C., and they have a new baby. We want to hire him here on the West Coast. I don't think I would have created a relationship to find out what the issues were when he was telling us he wasn't going to take the job; all this had come out in our discussions. His wife is in environmental science, but his PhD is very popular maybe here in the Bay Area or on the West Coast – not so popular on the East Coast and there's nothing in D.C. for him. We agreed that we would provide him round trip airfare for a year during her post-doc and he started last Monday.

Marcia: Part of that negotiation is figuring out what the company can provide in order to get that highly desirable candidate.

Joe: How do you overcome an objection if you don't know what the objection is?

Marcia: Exactly. It's a sales technique, overcoming an objection for something realistic that will help a candidate and close that deal.

Joe: I didn't try to force that. This is something that's outside of what our company can do. We can give you an opportunity, but you're going to have a personal life decision, it is up to you whether you take the job or not. We'll try to help you see it and if you think that works out for you, that you can live with that for a year, great – we would love to have you. If you can't, give us a call in a year and maybe we'll have an opening. There are no hard-sell tactics.   I don't want somebody at my door a month after we've hired him saying, "Why'd you talk me into this?" Or, the manager is at your door and the guy left after three months.

Marcia: You've worked as contractor and an in-house employee of companies, right?

Joe: Yes, I went over to the dark side once.

Marcia: What's the difference for you between working as a contractor and working as an employee?

Joe: It was only one company and there are some pluses and minuses. The minus is that if you're a contractor; a company will probably value your time a little bit more. They're not going to waste your time as much on, "Let's try this, if it doesn't work we can work Joe another 40 hours this week." That's one of the main reasons I don't like working in-house. I hate going to meetings because they cram 15 minutes worth of meeting into 4 hours; there's no beginning, no end, no action items. Most of the time – whatever time you want to call it – five o'clock on Friday - when you're done as a contractor, you go home and you can turn it off. You might make a few calls on the weekend to follow up with candidates, but as an employee I felt like Nikita Khrushchev banging my shoe on the table – why are we doing this stupid stuff?

Marcia: You also said that there are pluses to being an employee. What are some of the pluses?

Joe: I think you have a better chance of influencing things to make things better through hiring people.

Marcia: Do you report in to an HR Staffing Manager, or do you sometimes report in to an Engineering Director?

Joe: I have never reported to line management. Even when a VP hired me, I ended up reporting to an HR Senior Director. I supported the line guy, but I used all the policies and procedures of HR. You're going to have to hand off the person for boarding for new hire orientation, benefits, background checks, whatever it is – it's all intrinsic to HR.

Marcia: What was the most creative thing you've ever done to recruit someone?

Joe: A couple places that I've been to, even though they're multi-billion dollar companies, they have no college program. If I'm recruiting, I could put in a full-fledged college program, but I don't have time to go to universities to meet with the masses. Rather than that, I looked at the skill sets the company was hiring. What universities have specialized degrees or advanced research in those areas? Who are the professors doing that advanced research? I've created this grid, so when somebody says, "I'm looking for such and such," I find out if they need a new grad or PhD. I find three professors at three universities and that's three e-mails I have to send that ask, "Do you have a person who's going to be graduating or finishing their PhD over the next six months?" At one place I worked at for seven

70

months I made two hires from doing that. I never check on the college placement office.

Marcia: Do you have some candidates that spring to mind for the wrong reasons?

Joe: I find that Engineers are good at some things and bad at others. These days they don't expect an engineer to show up in a suit, but shorts and flip-flops? But yeah, it surprises me. The worst offenders are recruiters. The worst resume writers are recruiters. The worst interviewers are recruiters and they don't research the company that they're interviewing at. As a class, I would have to say that's the bottom of the totem pole.

Marcia: How would a candidate impress you?

Joe: Know something about the company. Go on the website and learn about the products, who we're selling to, what the products are, what a disc drive is if I'm applying at a disc drive company, or what a server is. You look it up on Wikipedia and you can go on Yahoo!, if it is a public company and there will be information about the stock and the health of the company, when such and such a company is in the news, here's a new CEO, and all that. [Press releases.] Just by 15 minutes of preparation candidates can get some basic knowledge and probably have a couple of decent questions.

Marcia: Do you have some advice for a person who's new to our business?

Joe: We just went through a recession again and we'll go through another one some time. I know that more than 80 percent of the recruiters that were employed in 2000 were unemployed in 2002. At the HRCA I did a straw poll and only 5 percent of them had jobs in recruiting. Some of them were selling washing machines at Sears. And you have to do what you have to do to keep the family together.

My advice would be if you're going to be a professional, treat it as a profession. Continually educate yourself and know that networking, whether you're a contract recruiter or in-house, is important. I've worked as a contract recruiter in-house, where they let the in-house recruiters go before they let me go; it was competency-based. You're going to compete with me for the job some day and I wish you luck on beating me out.

Marcia: Is there anything you'd like to add?

Joe: Yes: giving back. I've tried to go to some career fairs where they have a booth – HRCA, De Anza College, adult education does this – where we help people critique their resumes. That's also a point in networking, because other organizations are for people to network together looking for jobs. So don't be just a taker. Give something back, because what goes around comes around.

LINDA LOPEZ

Linda has worked in agency recruiting, has had a business placing technical contractors, and works as a contract recruiter. I first met her as my neighbor, became friends, and I've had the privilege of working with her. I have been impressed with her knowledge, her eagerness to learn, her creativity in sourcing and doggedness in working with sometimes difficult managers.

Marcia: How did you get into recruiting?

Linda: I have some college, and right after college I was a young mother. I like to be a people-person – so I was looking around for a position that had to do with perhaps sales or working with people. It had to be the kind of position that could scale up to have some potential for income since I was just starting out with my family. My ex-husband was involved in the computer industry and he had contacted this company to help them work on their VAX, which is an old computer technology. They had an opening for a recruiter/salesperson, so I applied and was able to be mentored. I learned quickly, and this was in 1986 – recruiting had a whole different face. I was targeting the aerospace industry because I lived in Southern California.

Marcia: How did you make the transition from college and being a young mother into the recruiting world? Was there some advice your mentor gave you, or did you watch and observe and mimic the mentor?

Linda: I came on board with this company and the owner and mentor was very dynamic – she was an ex-computer professional. She had taught computer professionals and then started this business where she placed contract programmers and engineers in the field. She was just a dynamo and I could relate to her and I was very eager to learn. My way of learning is through osmosis, so she handed me this big stack of accounts saying, "Here're all the managers for Hughes Aircraft. Call them and see if they want contract programmers." Well, what's a contractor? They put me through a little overview and I watched her and I went to sites with her. We used to have a routine we called the Barbara and Linda show, because we would meet with colonels and project managers and VPs of companies. I was 23, telling the colonels what to do and they'd say, "Stand down – what are you talking about? You really think I should hire this person?" These were colonels in the Air Force that we used to team with because we were a woman-owned business and they would hire us to fill out their projects. I learned about the process by just jumping right in.

I went to Colorado Springs and at the time we were a subcontractor. The Air Force was looking for somebody to work on their FAA flight craft control tower centers. They had several competing companies and in these projects they have a two-year-long rapid-prototyping phase. That means you would develop a whole system and present it on a bid so I learned all about bidding. We wanted to be on the winning team, of course, because after two years, if you win, you go on to build out all the FAA control centers. So you're trying to pick who's going to be the winning team. We went to the person who was deciding the winning team and presented ourselves as a young company. The government has certain set-asides for small businesses and that's what we were, so I also learned how to navigate government small businesses. At the same time I was soaking up the technology. I was really learning a lot and I applied the same techniques that I studied in school to the way I was studying my job.

I enjoyed going places and they said, "We have this project in Hawaii", and I said, "I'll take that one!" Next thing I know I'm on the plane going to Hawaii and visiting people at Boeing Aircraft. They were the government subcontractor that had the project for the computer control systems. Everyone's wearing Hawaiian shirts and we went to a Luau in celebration of all our people. I couldn't believe some of our programmers working on that project were actually complaining. So I kind of learned all the different levels and that was the first phase of my career.

Marcia: How long did you stay at the agency?

Linda: I worked there for seven years and then I came up to Northern California. We were moving away from aerospace - we had big accounts, one of them being NASA JPL, one of them being McDonnell-Douglas, which is now Boeing Aircraft, and I had worked on Boeing and Hughes Aircraft. All the aerospace companies seemed to merge with each other. We were moving to the commercial world and we had accounts like Disney, Taco Bell. Northern California – the Silicon Valley - was the place we had to be so I came up here with one of my partners and we were working diligently for a year. Moving to a new area and having a small office combined with going through a divorce – it was time to move on. I am still friends with the owner of that company; it's been 22 years since I've known her. I tried to emulate what I did there by starting my own agency with somebody I met there.

I had a Vietnamese partner and one of the projects we got was a Vietnamese contract with Sun, and we were supplying people to upgrade the Vietnamese ATMs. I continued with my recruiting efforts, working from home for two years with my partner, and our two biggest accounts were Visa and Sun. We didn't supply full-time contingency search; we supplied contractors. Those people were technically our employees, so we had to do a lot of paperwork and payroll and all those things that are involved in a business. I decided I didn't want to do that any more, so I sold that business back for its contracts. Since we had vendor agreements with Sun and Visa, it was pretty valuable and I sold that back to the agency that I worked for previously.

I met my neighbor, Marcia [the interviewer]; our sons were both named "Jason." The Jasons were playing and Marcia said, I'm a recruiter, and I said, I'm a recruiter, and she told me about contract recruiting. What contracting did is still allow me flexibility to go into companies and help them hire their regular full-time people and it opened a new world for me. I worked on my full first contract actually with Marcia at Silicon Gaming, which was a real-time gaming software company for the gambling industry. Not to be confused with video games, but it had the same kind of high tech video renderings on it. I got immersed in the corporate environment in the same way I did in the contract world, which is I really didn't know everything, but I just went in and learned through osmosis. It was the perfect company for me; I was there for 10 months.

Marcia: Where did you go next?

Linda: One of the things I was good at was working with companies that were in formation. I went to another startup; I actually was the first HR person onboard. They were doing some HR functions through the controller [finance] of the company. Oftentimes, new companies will have the finance department run HR, but there're a lot of things in HR and recruiting is only one aspect, and within recruiting there're a lot of aspects. You have to convince the company that recruiting is not just about finding people; recruiting has to do with retention, it has to do with succession planning, it has to do with legal processes to implement as your company grows. When we first started, this particular company didn't have a lot of things in place despite a very seasoned controller he really didn't have the HR background.

Marcia: How did you learn HR?

Linda: I went to meetings, I took some classes, I read some books and again, I learned through osmosis and through doing, so I asked a lot of people things, and I did a lot of reading. I've always taken my study skills to my job. And with the Internet now it's easy to find information.

Recruiting has changed from pre-Internet days. I started in 1986 - that definitely was in pre-Internet days - and it was all about keeping a lot of stuff in your head because even the PCs weren't that great, so you didn't have large databases. At any given time I might know two or three thousand names. To this day my friend will still call me up from 22 years ago – remember that guy that worked at Lockheed, we met him on the tarmac, and I'm like, Oooh! But you come across the same names, because in this business I've actually come across the same people that I've known from many years ago.

Marcia: How many years have you been contracting now?

Linda: Since 1996. So it would be 11 years as a contractor and during that time I didn't have contracts for about 2 years.

Marcia: We had a recession when recruiters were looking for something to do.

Linda: That's probably a year and a half, but basically there were down times – that's what I loved about contracting, because I did take off two months to go skiing in 1998. It was a way to make money and I was able to take a long-time sabbatical to do things like that. I've looked at my career and usually I took my vacations in between my assignments. I've been contracting at this company for two years and I take vacation at various times but I don't get paid for that vacation. I usually take time off and work that into the hiring trends.

Marcia: What are the differences between being an agency recruiter and being a contract recruiter?

Linda: Working onsite at a company exposes you to the issues of the company. You have the same kind of interest as an employee: you get involved in their releases of their software, their success when a new customer signs, new product lines, new ventures, you're caught up in the corporate culture. If you like a sense of corporate pride, you do get that sense of really being involved and having a stake in your recruiting, as opposed to working externally where you're just trying to please your customer.

When you're on the outside, there're pluses and minuses to that. I liked being on the outside, because my attention at the time was focused on learning new technologies and I didn't really have to understand all the issues that were going on within each of my clients, other than how it related to filling their requisitions.

Marcia: If someone is looking at agency recruiting and at contract recruiting, do you have any words of wisdom for them?

Linda: There are actually three things: being an agency recruiter, being a contract consulting recruiter, and being a full-time in-house recruiter, which I haven't been. Being a full-time in-house recruiter can be a good entry-level position, the same as with an agency position. Both of them give you a little time to ramp up. I think that's really important when you're first starting out. I would definitely say that working within a company as a full-time contract recruiter – whenever you're a consultant – you have to really hit the ground running.

Being an in-house recruiter, you're subject to the trends that hit that company, so you have to focus more on which company am I going to choose and what's that going to do for my career.

If you like being in the car, you like going out to lunches, you like meeting with your clients, you like hearing about new stuff and you like "go, go, go!" being in an agency can be fun. The drawback with being in an agency is you don't get the same amount of feedback. You feel a little bit out of control, but if one customer falls through, you go on to the next, and you don't really have to stake your whole heart in one company.

Choosing an agency can really help you learn a lot of different technologies and help you see what you might be interested in. You might not be interested in technology. You might be interested in working with cancer research, biotech instrumentation, or recruiting for types of jobs in the fashion industry or in the film industry.

As far as some global words of wisdom: no matter where you go, be true to yourself. Recruiting is an area that gets stretched, bent, it moves into a lot of different directions, and you've got to follow your intuition. There's a code of ethics. You're jostling against other companies, you're trying to get the best candidates and no matter who talks to you about it, whether it's a VP in the company, the CTO or the CEO or your immediate boss – it's sometimes hard to say no. Always go with your gut feel and if it is contrary to the chain of command, have the reasons ready why you think it should be a certain way that might be different than what they're saying.

Have fun with your work, because recruiting is also a job that no matter what, you're never going to be done. It's not the kind of job where you can get a certain amount of things done – like your dishwasher. That's a very rudimentary kind of analogy – but at the end of the day a mechanic does so many cars; you wash so many dishes. You might complete projects – when you're looking at a high-end project manager within a company, there's always a project to start and complete. There are certain lines and milestones within recruiting that you complete and it means you're filling a position. But you're always going to have more positions to fill and there's always going to be another task. So don't get too stressed out, don't try to do it too much, try to pace yourself. I've now been recruiting since 1986, so that makes 21 years of recruiting and you're just never done. I'm also never bored. That's my advice for recruiters.

Marcia: When you do contract work, you're always looking for the next job. How do you market yourself?

Linda: There're different ways that I've found jobs. When you're starting out it's really good to go to meetings. There're all different kinds of network meetings, there are luncheons, and there are focus groups in your industry. For example, all the biotech recruiters kind of get together at a biotech meeting. There are different organizations that are more global, it might actually be targeted to the industry or targeted to recruiting. If you're in, say, architecture and energy, you're going to go to maybe these architecture and energy seminars and you're going to meet people saying, "I need somebody to help me hire XYZ."

The other thing is to have your close personal contacts. I've gotten more referrals from my close contacts than anything. Our economy is really picking up in terms of hiring, so posting an updated resume on the job boards with a clear-cut objective would be very important, because the recruiter's going to look at what does this person want to do. If you're just getting out of school, write your resume so that it includes the kinds of classes you've worked on and the kinds of projects you completed. If you've been in a class that would be relevant towards the field you want to go into, don't talk about necessarily your fast-food experience, even though it's nice that you held down a job for five years while you were in college; talk about what you studied while you were in college.

In the world of recruiting, learning skills like Excel, understanding the computer, learning Boolean search skills – those kinds of things are really important now, because the Internet has a vast amount of places to search for resumes. It's a lot different than when we had to cold call into companies or run advertisements in newspapers. There're all sorts of social on-line networking groups; people use MySpace for recruiting.

Marcia: Do you have a word of advice for MySpace users?

Linda: For MySpace, as in anything, you don't want to tell personal information – don't throw your resume up on MySpace. But you can say if your interests are in a particular area and you're interested in getting in to that, then people can contact you and you're back to using your gut feel, because it's all about making contact with that person. The Internet is a tool to be able to source and to connect. Relying on that as a way to shield you from actually talking to that person and making a real human connection is not the way to go.

Marcia: Do you have some advice for candidates in general?

Linda: For candidates I would say knowledge is power. When you are deciding what companies you might want to get into, what kinds of jobs you might want to do, you can look up things, you can Google it, learn as much as you can about the company before you go there. Sometimes companies won't give you a job description but ask for one. Update your resume and read through it. Understand your resume so if they ask about what you've done, you will be able to elaborate on it, you will be able to explain. If you can't, take it off your resume. You don't really need fluff on your resume. Companies really like a lot of things on the resume that are actually what you've done.

From the technical standpoint, I've heard from a lot of managers they'd rather interview someone based on what they've done, even if it's not exactly what the company is looking for and see how well they've done what they've done. If you're programming in Java, they'll ask you about a language that you know really well, and then may ask you to solve a technical problem in that language. Maybe it's not what they're using at their company. So definitely know yourself and know the company where you're going.

Marcia: Do you have anything to add?

Linda: I would really like to emphasize the fun stuff. Recruiting has been lucrative for me. It can be very lucrative in the world of start-ups and getting stock options, but you know, the old adage of "do what you love and the money will come" – that's really what I say. If you're not passionate about what you're doing and you don't enjoy it, don't do it for the money, it'll just be a grind.

80

Tamara Swearingen

Tamara has worked in retail, in agency recruiting, and as a contract recruiter in the Silicon Valley and the East Bay. She has mentored many recruiters and utilized her good customer service skills in her work.

Tamara: I live in Livermore Valley [Northern California] and I'm a Senior Technical Contract Recruiter.   My first career was in retail management as a children's buyer in San Francisco where I had so much fun interacting with customers. I switched from being an HR manager/retail manager and decided to go into fashion consulting. I worked for some predominant retail companies and had a career in that for about 12 years. I ended up taking classes at San Francisco Community College and was given an opportunity at I. Magnin. I was promoted to children's buyer for all west coast stores and the central region. I did that for two and a half years and loved it, but I felt like I had reached my plateau.

A friend had been hired from a company called Drake International, which was an agency that was coming to San Francisco. She asked me to help her set up an office and ended up being there a couple years. We built up the office that was temp to perm and direct hire and I enjoyed it. I had a chance to work with people in customer service and deal with managers and customers. I helped people find jobs as opposed to finding them clothes.

Marcia: Did they train you to be a recruiter?

Tamara: I went through business development classes, managerial classes, women in management classes and found an area that I was really interested in. I worked for Drake International as well as four other employment agencies and was interested in the computer world, i.e. DP/MIS (management information systems/data processing), which at that point was the beginning of high technology. I decided I would teach myself more about the industry and what could I do to break into it since I wanted to be a corporate recruiter.   At that point we weren't thinking of contract recruiting as it is today. I did a lot of asking questions: how come, why, what, where and how?

Marcia: These were informational interviews - who did you talk with?

Tamara: I was a member of the Chamber of Commerce. I got involved in professional associations but people I knew were connected in the industry. I got in touch with some people that had a company in the Silicon Valley and we started talking about my career and if I wanted to stay in the agency industry. I got my first project job (contract) and since then have worked for the last 18 years in the Silicon Valley placing technical and non-technical candidates in high technology sectors. A couple of people took me under their wing and thought, here's somebody who's hungry, who is teaching herself and interviewing people about what it takes to get into the industry, reading magazines about the high technology sector like PC World, reading jargon I didn't know anything about, and talking to engineers and asking questions like what's GUI - is that really something gooey? - and learning that it's Graphical User Interface.

Over a year and a half, I wanted to know more about the HR community. The foundation I received working for a couple of employment agencies really got me grounded because I had the door closed on me on the phone. I had people say, "No, we don't want to work with you" and "What makes you so much better than this agency?" It gave me a chance to start consulting with people as to why Drake International or Snelling & Snelling was good.

Marcia: When you're at an agency, you have to call people to try and get business, so you have to toughen yourself for rejection. You might sometimes have a "yes" or "no thanks" and sometimes some rude comments.

Tamara: By the same token some people were saying, "Thank you so much! Wow, you gave me more information than I've heard from somebody that has called from your office before because you took the time and let me know what you had to share. You listened to what was important to me and what I needed. Because of that we want to work with you." I realized that I could work elsewhere if I applied that technique, so my style was to consult with people. I had a chance to go to Hewlett Packard and IBM and Space Systems/Loral and I ended up working in many work environments. The last 18 years I've been very happy and proud to know people that believed in what I could bring to the table, helped me, mentored me and saw I was somebody that was really hungry to know more about HR and recruiting. These people saw I was going to add value working with customers and defining and being that liaison between candidates and managers to help candidates get hired and help managers get work off their plates.

Marcia: These companies had technologies they were developing and selling and you also had different technologies internally to work with as a recruiter. How did you keep track of all of these technologies?

Tamara: It was nice to be able to go from one business unit or the concept of what the company was about to different work environments like e-business, e-commerce, or government since it didn't matter what the work environment was. Sometimes in interviews at these different companies they would get caught up in the fact that I didn't have the work experience in government, telecommunications or semi-conductor. What I impressed upon them is that as a seasoned contract recruiter it's about understanding the managers' needs.

Once I got the managers to understand that I knew the menu of a really good seasoned recruiter, they then gave me a chance. After several contracts it wasn't an issue any more – they looked at my resume and realized somebody gave me the opportunity and believed in me. Every company had their own menu of what you're supposed to do to attract candidates and the hire ratio, which was really important. We assessed what outside resources we needed to have onsite, corporate recruiters and contract recruiters. We looked at every requisition and what was forecasted in the budget. It is funny how much we educated managers that not every requisition [financially] allowed outside resources [agencies] to be part of the hiring process. I never wanted to be a contract recruiter and sit there as a glorified paper-pusher for agencies. I tried to build credibility with managers and relationship-building and how can we work together so that we wouldn't have to use outside resources and explain this is how I track candidates. A lot of times a company would have support people but there were times there wasn't a support person; you set up the interviews, put the offer letters together, type them and give them out. It was a luxury when you go to another company and there was a person that you could give the interview schedule to and they'd set it up and track what candidates were coming in against what req. All you had to do was worry about sourcing and finding the suitable candidate that fit the culture, matched the skill sets, but also had the chemistry or personality.

I would sit with the manager and ask questions like, "Besides the requisition, what's your group like? What's the personality? I need to understand who you are as a manager, what your expectations are in this individual. Is the group serious or do they like to laugh? I'm looking at the skill sets but I also need to find the right personality, because if that chemistry is not there among the people on your team, it's not going to work out. If you want a credible, long-lasting relationship with your team and everybody's working together on different tasks to get that project completed and in a timely fashion, it's got to work all the way around." Most managers will have specific people on their team that have a little niche. We look at a candidate as a piece of a puzzle, because when they are put together with other puzzle pieces the team can be completed. It's only complete one day, because two days later one of those puzzle pieces is giving her notice.

I go where I know I can bring some deliverables to the table. When you're invited back a second time like I have been through my career that to me is credible. I've gone back six places a second time since I developed a good relationship with managers.

You're going to have different candidates: the new college grad; the people that are very business savvy who've been in the industry for a couple of years; senior level directors all the way to the executive level. The fortunate thing for us is that you still listen to a need of a candidate and what they're looking for and what's their growth opportunity.

You go to a manager in order to understand their business needs, not only for the current quarter but for the next three to six months. You ask questions like, "What's your forecast? Have you thought about building a pipeline of candidates we can tap into?" Or perhaps they know people and there's a referral.

When we go into a contract we need to know that we're full service [full-service] people that help make a difference. Are we viewed as an onsite recruiter or employee? We do a lot of the same work, but we're more under the microscope. We're paid a bit more than the average on-site corporate recruiter. We are there for a period of time and we don't get benefits or stock unless it's part of a package that's been agreed upon in our contract. We're there in an escalation moment, hired for areas that need people pretty fast. Typically we work under a three- to six-month contract time but when we get that contract extended we know they're happy with us. Sometimes contracts may not work out and they may not be a fit or the business goes in a different direction.

Marcia: Did you have a hard time when you first started contract recruiting and you didn't want to leave but it was time?

Tamara: The nice thing is those were the companies that invited me back so we looked at it as a turnkey. You go back in and ask, "What's changed? What's new? What did we get rid of?" Then you're on your way. Those were great contracts because I already knew the processes and procedures. If there were enhancements, that was great.

A contract recruiter, sourcer or anybody in our field has to be creative and get people to buy in, listen and teach people. I didn't realize how many people I had taught and mentored. I remember that I would look at people in HR and say, "Gee, I'd like to be like you, how did you get there?" I asked a lot of questions to people that took me under their wing and taught me and gave me an opportunity. Now in the last couple of years people come up to me and say, "Tamara! I've been wanting to meet you!"

I was at a recruiter's luncheon that was the 10-year anniversary of somebody [Susan Welch] that dedicated and gave her time putting on luncheons for us to network, focus on topics, be educated, then help us when we needed a contract or advice. It was great to be part of that original recruiter luncheon of 13 people and now seeing 700 people that are part of this major luncheon and event that happens once a month. I stood at the front, looking at a lot of new faces, but also a lot of faces that were very recognizable and had been in the valley longer than me. I realized I was one of those seasoned people. Now I've got three people who want to talk with me and teach them things such as new areas of HR, recruiting and sourcing, and what HR is all about and how did I get into it.

Marcia: How do you find new contracts aside from the repeats?

Tamara: My strongest advice for everybody is networking. Don't burn your bridges and stay in communication with people. We're so fortunate to have many professional associations, Yahoo! groups, women's organizations and people who have dedicated time to give us a chance to network. There are no excuses not to stay connected with people. During my last couple of assignments I've had people reach out to me because I had a reputation I had built. Keep the networking strong because word travels very fast. If you bring good things to the table and your deliverables, people are going to want that. We need to teach people that "good" means customer service, networking and the fundamentals.

Marcia: How do you determine your rate?

Tamara: I don't let the pay rate drive where I go to on a contract. I always have the question, "What areas do I want to be recruiting in?" My passion is recruiting across the board. It doesn't matter if it's hardware, software, marketing, sales or finance. I want to know where there's a manager that doesn't believe in HR because I know I can have a success story or two to tell when I leave that contract. My rate has been based on my deliverables, the places I've worked at and the length of time. I set my rate where I won't go below. There comes a point in time when you have earned the right to be a senior recruiter and that's not always by a title. Don't let titles steer you.

Employers will pay me when they look at my past, what I brought to the table and that I know what I'm talking about. I go for the opportunity and then the salary. The hourly rate has been secondary but it comes first if there's a long commute.

Marcia: There are some people who think, "All I have to do is join this group and I will then be assured of continued job links and information flowing my way." Could you talk a little bit about their responsibility to their network?

Tamara: Building your network is the complete opposite of that. I hear this all the time that people think that's all they need to do. You can't hide behind a forum or a job board or anything that's seamless. You have to let people know who you are and get out there and let people talk to you face to face. Take time and go to luncheons, dinners, give a speech about the company that you're currently representing, go to a professional association. It doesn't take a lot of time to do that and you have to keep that up.

Getting your resume posted doesn't really give people a chance to know who you are. You have to be persistent. You can't sit and wait for the phone to ring. A recruiter's going to notice a candidate who's persistent, who sells themselves on the phone, because they know a resume only does so much and a phone call only does so much. If they're persistent, sometimes a recruiter will say, "I've got to call this candidate back." We love to see the person who's not giving up, who says, "You've got to see me, you've got to meet me." There's more to my resume. Nine times out of 10 those are the people that I will usually call first.

I have always been a dedicated recruiter that gets back to every single candidate. That's their resume: I acknowledge it when it's been received. There are recruiters that say they don't have time. I think if they have time to open a resume and read it, then have the courtesy to get back to a candidate and let them know it was received. It doesn't take that much time.

Because recruiters have been on the other side of the table, we know what it's like when you don't hear from a recruiter. It's not good customer service and not a good perception of the company. We hear about the black hole all the time. I hear candidates saying, "I never get a response back from recruiters. Thank you so much for responding even though it was a 'no.' It was a live message and not the same message sent to over 50 people." Tell them a resume is not a fit after an interview and send them a handwritten note. I send those personalized thank you cards or no thank you cards. Many people say if they weren't a fit for a job, please keep them in mind, because if this is an example of what the company is about then this is the place where they want to work.

Marcia: Are there certain qualities recruiters ought to have, and what advice would you give a new recruiter?

Tamara: Make sure that this is the industry you want to go into. How do you know? You should have some conversations with people who've been in the industry for a while and ask them, "Why did they choose to go into the industry? What are the pitfalls, what is the upside?" Become knowledgeable and be passionate. Passion is believing in what you bring to the table – your deliverables. Know what it takes to be a recruiter. Don't be afraid to teach yourself things about it. Investigate and read books.

You need to have good customer service and patience. You're going to be dealing with customers who may not always be nice.

You cannot take things personally. Understand there's frustration on the hiring manager's side. If you go down one road and that fails as far as your strategy to find people, don't give up. I'd like new recruiters to really understand what they're getting into and not be afraid to ask questions and talk to professionals in the industry to become more knowledgeable. One day they won't be the protégé, they'll be the mentor.

Marcia: Do you have a list of dos and don'ts or pet peeves about candidates?

Tamara: Really read the job posting and understand the position and if it is a fit against your skill sets. What's been frustrating for me, especially the last couple of years, is there has been an abundance of candidates sending their resumes that don't fit the requirements. They're thinking they can send their resume over just to get in the door. Recruiters at companies don't have time to consult with each person and tell them they don't qualify. There are some candidates that submit their resume and they are not a fit whatsoever and you wonder: Why did they even send it? It looks like they responded to the wrong job. I want candidates to really understand that recruiters are not your enemy. Try to build a relationship with them, because that's what they want to do with you. Let the recruiter know what you want to be doing, not only for this job, but beyond. What are your salary requirements? The last thing you need to do is inflate your salary just because you think you're deserving of a raise. The recruiter has the resources to go back and find out what you made and you don't want any embarrassing moments.

The recruiter is going to look out for your best interest. If you put your cards on the table, you're going to have a very rewarding relationship with that recruiter and that will go even further with having a chance to interview with the hiring manager. Present yourself in the best fashion, come across smart and show what really made you choose this industry. That recruiter will give a nice presentation to the manager hoping it will result in an interview. Don't come across overly aggressive and don't come across like you're a know-it-all; be truly you. Be polished and presentable and don't wear bad, ripped clothes that are wrinkled. Be sure to have good hygiene. We look back on instances where we had to tell a candidate, "You need to wash your hair. You need to bathe. You need to come as a professional. You look like you put yourself together in five minutes. Did you brush your teeth?" I mean, these are common sense things.

You're representing yourself, so when you come to an interview, make sure that you've done research such as looked at the website. Recruiters and managers love candidates who have taken the time to look at the buyers and executives. Know what the products are, what the mission statement is and in what direction the company is going. I've had candidates that told me who the competitors were. Those are the candidates that have taken the time to put together what we're doing and they're prepared to add value to the company. It's finding the right job and a good fit. Show up to an interview looking like somebody wants to just hire you right on the spot and have you start that day. Are you dressed for success?

Marcia: Recruiters who've been around have seen down times in our economy. I don't think that there was a worse time than following the dotcom bust – there were recruiters who were leaving the industry, leaving the community. What would you advise recruiters to do to prepare for those times?

Tamara: That was a horrible time. There were a lot of people that jumped into the HR field and called themselves a recruiter during the dotcom boom. A lot of companies weren't really aware how valuable seasoned recruiters can be. They soon realized that if they hire an entry-level recruiter, after a while of being on assignment they really didn't bring the deliverables. A lot of seasoned recruiters did leave; it was time for them to retire and they wanted to get out of the business. The dotcom bust cleaned house and got rid of a lot of people that wanted to do recruiting. The recruiters that went through that period of time did everything possible to survive. We got creative in trying to keep our heads above water.

It could never be the roller coaster ride that we rode back then. It was an incredible time for all of us – very fast paced with a lot of things going on. I think it woke up not only recruiters in the industry or people wanting to get in, but companies were forced without having a lot of employees to do cross-training. It was an added value for a lot of people that didn't have a chance to know what it was like to work in staffing, who worked in recruiting and then all of a sudden recruiters became sourcers, too. We always were sourcing, but we never brought it as a separate job. So there were new things that came out of that and as soon as we started getting back on track, companies became more self-sufficient in cross-training and they didn't need to hire as many people. When they hired people in HR, contract recruiters were brought in because they were seasoned.

For recruiters in the industry now, I would advise them to be aware that it's not always going to be good times. Brace yourself, don't throw in the towel, keep yourself energized, do whatever thing you can do to keep yourself involved with recruiting. This has happened a couple times – not as bad as in 2000 – but it happened in previous years. I've gone through this three times. There's still recruiting but you have to seek out activity.

You are going to make your career. You create your growth, your prosperity and your future. HR is such a wonderful, large world of opportunity. Be smart, be business savvy, stay a couple steps ahead of somebody else. If you find yourself "existing" in recruiting it's probably not the area you need to be in. You'll know because you're energized about it and as long as you keep that, you'll instill that in other people and it will be a great work environment.

I'm glad I chose the profession. I'm glad I had the chance to be on my own at 17 in my first apartment in San Francisco. I taught myself in a lot of things and I never expected to have anything handed to me. We're given one life and you have to create what it is you want to do. If you choose HR, you'll find yourself in a career that can keep expanding for many years. Keep abreast of things, keep yourself educated, keep up on the technology, keep developing those business relationships with managers and keep getting back to candidates.

I've helped rewrite resumes so many times it's not even funny, but you get thanks from somebody saying, "Nobody ever took the time to do that. Thank you for getting back and telling me that this is the reason why I didn't get the job, because now I can learn, I can better myself." Don't get into politics.

If you can mentor others, take the time to add value to somebody else's life. Touch somebody else's heart and spend a few moments with somebody that's elderly. Don't be afraid to smile because it can make somebody's day. When you work in a very fast-paced work environment, human resource people give the human touch. The simple things that we can do to enhance somebody else's life can be all the difference for the right direction in their career path.

Recruiters - always treat candidates fairly and teach them what you can. Today's candidate is tomorrow's vice president or CEO. You may get a call from the CEO who says, "Do you remember me? You took the time to take care of me when I was a candidate; you educated me and how you are with me is what I want you to do. Come work for me. You made me realize that my destiny is up to me."

Today's work with people will be remembered down the way. They remember those people that took the opportunity to help them rewrite that resume or coach them on their career path, or give them some insight that they never thought about. That's what makes the successful consultant or HR professional. If we give that human touch, we've done our job.

3

STAFFING DIRECTORS

Aanand Murthy Varanasi
Aanand has experience in sales, has worked in search/research and has worked at an employment agency. His love of recruiting has resulted in his position as the Director of Global Staffing at VMware in Palo Alto, California.

Aanand: I'm the Director of Global Staffing at VMware where I've worked for four and a half years. We've got about 110 or a 115 people in staffing – heavy duty in outbound methodologies – tapping into building relationships with the passive and waiting for the passive/active candidate.

My father is a physicist. He comes from a family of seven brothers and a sister, I think five of which are doctors. I assumed I would be a scientist or a doctor. I went to UC (University of California) San Diego and was a cell biology major. When it came time to graduate I realized I wasn't going to be a scientist. I didn't have the aptitude – I'd worked in labs. I went through a number of years trying to figure out what I was good at and what I wasn't good at. I spent the majority of my twenties in jobs that I wouldn't have been good at.

Marcia: What kinds of jobs?

Aanand: I worked in labs for biotech companies and I went from there to sales. I was a field sales person on my own in Chicago and I still associated myself much more with scientists than salespersons, which I didn't like myself. There was an Indian woman who was in the biotech company that I worked for and because we were just about the only two Indians in the company, I confided in her that I didn't like what I was doing. I liked a lot of sales, I liked the people orientation and I'm very competitive, but I did not like being treated as a door-to-door salesman type of person, and that's how I saw myself. She said, "You should talk to the people that recruit our scientists. It probably involves a lot of the skills that you like, but you're not a sales person – you're not treated as a sales person," at least not in her understanding.

I went to work for this agency. They were a couple of crooks – I hated them, but I learned the business and I really liked it. I went from there and bounced around and ended up being a sourcer or researcher for a number of people.

Marcia: How did they train you?

Aanand: They had some sort of job analysis form they would start out with that gave researchers the targets. I went to archives in universities and libraries trying to figure out who was doing what and looking up patents and old types of research. I tried to figure out who were the ones that had the green thumbs in these biological markets, the people that had built successful operations and very specific technologies. Sometimes they weren't the technologists themselves that had discovered it, especially in a production world versus a pure R&D world. You had to figure out who was successful, not just who knew the science and who built labs that had yields. For instance, in monoclonal diagnostics, who had put the first monoclonal programs together for the first cancer research companies. I started to go and figure it out and I love that part. I was thinking about it just the other day: The thing that I like that I don't do enough of any more is the puzzle and I love a puzzle I can go into for hours and even days. Now there are just so many transactions in my world that I never go deep into the puzzle.

Marcia: When you were doing research, did you do the profiling too, where you would call up the candidate and find out a bit about them?

Aanand: Over time I did every aspect of it, I think. Initially, no. The nickname from my first job was called a longlister.

Marcia: What's a longlister?

Aanand: As a longlister I would take a job analysis form that would have technologies, labs, target companies and I would have to come up with the list of maybe a hundred names. In some cases there were only 12 names and that was the long list. Then the senior recruiter or partner would take that from the longlist down to the four best and available interested people in market to create the shortlist. I did everything from research to profiling. Actually I had done some contract recruiting before going there. I ended up doing research profiling and I think at one time I had 13 researchers and/or profilers that were working in my group.

You know, sometimes that part of the business is not something you can easily talk about, especially in this world of pretexting and what happened at HP, but I really enjoyed some of that work. I think today, a good ruse is –

Marcia: We should explain what a ruse is.

Aanand: There are all kinds of ruses – and I think the one that recruiters know best is to call a company and say, "Oh, I'm so thankful your VP of Engineering helped me out. My car was broken down on the side of the road, he gave me his card, but I've misplaced it. All I remember is he was your VP of Engineering and I just want to relay my thanks."

Marcia: I've always had this question: as you're rusing all day, do you start to feel bad about it, because you're making up stories to people all day?

Aanand: Yes, well, there are all kinds of ruses, and so there are all kinds of crumby ones that really play off of a lot of things.

The school of recruiting that I come from is that the best people out there do not e-mail resumes over a corporate Internet and apply for jobs. They don't go to job fairs. If and when they're looking, they mention it to a few people in their network and then offers come and they may not even produce a resume. So I highly believe in that outbound methodology and that's what we've built here.

It's how we got agencies out; we haven't used an agency in more than three years and it's because we've built a solid, strong partnership by disclosing our methodologies and doing lots of homework to find out who are the best people before we go and seek them. The best people know the best people and we're building all kinds of tools – communities to build relationships with all those best people in market relative to the skill sets that we look for.

Marcia: What do you mean by building community?

Aanand: Right now we've got a couple of things that we do. We've set up a website. You could call it a landing site or a micro-site that is all about working for VMware. It's not, "Please apply for this job", it's about who we are, what we're working towards, what our values are, what intrigues us about the technical challenges here, and about our technology itself. We try to bring people to this landing page just to keep in touch and build a relationship and let them know when we have tech talks, let them know some of the new things and ideas that are perplexing us, build relationships with key people internally, so they can keep in touch.

Marcia: Are the tech talks done via webinars?

Aanand: We do both online and physical. We just opened up an engineering facility in Boulder, Colorado. When we started there we did a massive marketing campaign to engineers relevant to the skill sets that we wanted to employ there. I don't think there's an engineer in the State of Colorado that didn't get contacted by us. We did a tech talk: "VMware is moving to Colorado, these are the different ideas that we're working on, these are the different labs that we're going to have, these are the different products and technologies that we'll be focused on.

We're going to have a number of these different talks put on by our thought leaders here at VMware. Please come and just help us think about our technologies, understand some of our challenges, where we think we're going." Then we said, "Oh, by the way, we are hiring and we are having a hiring event and if you're interested this is what you do, or if you want to tell someone else."

We would send them to our landing page and then we know where they came from. They can opt in and say, "I am this kind of engineer, but I'm not at all interested now, give me nine months," or "That location doesn't work for me, but if you think you might be doing something over here, let me know." We then can break these people down into units or verticals and say, these are our OS (operating systems) kernel people, these are our apps (applications) people, these are our storage people – engineers all, but you could apply this to any skill set. Then we can re-campaign to them later, or get in touch with them in a time frame in which they are interested, or keep them apprised of certain things that develop in the technologies of our company, build relationships, make them aware, keep them involved, be in the front of their mind when they do decide they want to make a change.

Marcia: When you mentioned building relationships, some of the larger companies match up potential candidates with employees, so that employees can kind of mentor them through the process. Is that what you do?

Aanand: We don't have recruiters in the communities. We've picked a number of our best employees that speak best for our values and technologies. We have blogging, we have newsletters, we have opt-in e-mail marketing, so we can understand what people are interested in, what their timing is and what their background is. They can build relationships with certain people that work on specific types of projects or products and we can understand what they're interested in. It's all about capturing – keeping in touch with the passive candidate, and then capturing information on them specific to their timing and interests and other relevant things, all with their permission so that when we have something that is of their interest we can give it to them.

Marcia: Your department is tracking a lot of different candidates. What kind of software do you use to do that? How do you keep on top of the latest?

Aanand: We have something that goes back to my agency days and I call it a PTS – Prospect Tracking System. It's tied to our landing page – that community. When people opt in and leave us information, it goes into our PTS and we have our own research group here. All they do is generate news for us worldwide that goes into the PTS. (Please see the Glossary.) Interestingly enough, there are two sides of the PTS: one is that I can look at the ROI [return on investment] on prospects that we generate by source – whether they come from the landing page or research or LinkedIn, and the recruiters themselves have LinkedIn. I've got like 90 categories of source in the PTS. I can also see which recruiters are e-mailing, leaving messages, tracking and various steps through the work flow as they get them to candidate development and get a resume and connect them with a job or a job req number.

Then they flip them over to another system, which is an ATS [Applicant Tracking System], and that's Trovix. I tried to develop my own ATS here, because I hate all ATSs, because they don't represent real work flow to me and don't provide good analysts. They might cover you for compliance, but I hate all of them. My challenge was that I was building my own ATS and trying to get IT to support it and struggling and flailing; engineering started attracting candidates on their own through an adaptation of Budzilla, which didn't cover us for compliance. I didn't own it, so it was a nightmare since engineering owned it. Trovix has this neat, fuzzy logic that was developed at MIT. The engineers here loved the smart technology that it had, which we truly benefit very little from. But the engineers loved it, so it allowed me to implement it. Trovix was a start-up and I said I'll be your reference customer, but you need to give me workflow that works for me. We're still developing it.

98

Marcia: What do you look for when you're looking for recruiters, and what advice would you give to someone who wants to be a recruiter?

Aanand: I truly believe in what I call the staffing partner model and I think that very few recruiters really attain that. By understanding your customer's business thoroughly, you get to the point where you don't just look at a resume and say, "looks good – send it." You look at that resume, screen the candidate against the business requirements and rank them. Because that screen is a living document, you don't get it right the first time. Let's say you're a manager, I'm a recruiter, we sit down and we develop this screen – maybe you don't know the job that well, so the screen has to be redone a little further as you learn – but if I screen this candidate very deeply and by an agreed-upon screen, it should go into your calendar. That is the amount of vetting that you've asked for. When there's a point where you're talking to people that are not appropriate, you need to get back in touch with me and we need to redevelop that screen.

That doesn't happen at most companies. Recruiters send resumes, they've answered a few questions and the manager then decides whether they will or they won't talk to them and that doesn't work very well. That's the most fundamental step in building a partnership, but it goes all the way through hire. I tell all the recruiters here I want to get to the point where you screened that candidate and you decide if they come in to interview or not.

I want us to get even better than that. I want to get to the point where 50 percent of the people you bring in get hired. Too many people fumble and leave it at lower steps where managers can turn around and say, "doesn't meet my spec" – they don't have to say why. I believe in that partnership and it's the ability to communicate and influence that gets you there.

Marcia: We were talking offline about research and the way recruiters look at the Internet.

99

Aanand: There are so many neat tools on the Internet that you end up with Internet Recruiters and Researchers ["flip searchers" or "flippers"].   When I took this job full time, one of my first tasks was to build our own research department so I could manage them first hand. I can have metrics and I can rate them by specific performance.

I put flip searchers next to rusing researchers over the phone. And a good ruse – you know, you don't tell the side of the freeway thing. A really good ruse goes undetected. If you were going to call in VMware, you would find out who the VMware partners are. EMC owns VMware, and you figure out somebody who works in the CTO's office and you come up with an undetectable ruse that has urgency where it's very hard to discern. Those are the fun ruses to put together and you have to spend a couple hours on them. When you put them together and deliver it, you're going to get names.   When I put these rusing researchers next to flip searchers, I got better quality and quantity, and I decided to not use flip searchers anymore.   Not everything is on the Internet.

The same thing goes to recruiting and that's part of the reason I have the PTS. Back to what I said about developing that partnership, doing a deep vet or a deep screen based on the understanding that you've developed with your hiring managers. Too many recruiters look at a resume, forward the resume and think it's all quantitative and not qualitative.   They come here and recruiters don't want to screen people or pick up the phone. They don't want to meet with the manager and get deeper and better with that telephone screen.

I always tell my recruiters, if someone's close by, do the screen face to face. Tell them it's a half an hour and ask them to come in. You learn so much more. I get too many recruiters that want to do it all over the Internet without a telephone call, without communication, even with their hiring managers. Even some of the ATSs now have ranking systems where the ATS will come up with the best candidates, but they can only take it so far. There's no substitute to a telephone conversation or face-to-face conversation for the recruiter and the candidate, or for the recruiter and the hiring manager. With this PTS, I want to see how many telephone conversations they had before they develop the candidate. In the ATS, I want to see that they do a screen with every candidate. I never want a candidate forwarded without a telephone screen and if possible, I'd like to see it done face-to-face, otherwise you can't get better at it. It becomes self-limited.

Marcia: Do you feel there's an X-factor that's in a candidate that provides that candidate a boost over other equally qualified candidates?

Aanand: There are always the empirical factors based on the work you've done and the work that you can illustrate that you've done on your resume, but I think communication skills, presentations skills and likeability play a lot into it.

It's the same thing I look for in my recruiters. If you call someone up and you're personable, listen and articulate, you're a lot less likely to have a telephone hung up on you. We have very simple data that we can get out of our ATS to show which recruiters are the most productive and so I look at higher productivity. You hand-select some of the best recruiters and you go back to the PTS and you find out what are the attributes and what do they do. You find out if they place a lot more phone calls and so it's communication skills. I don't want to hire a recruiter that fears the phone. I think there are lots of recruiters that fear the phone.

Marcia: That early sales experience that you have might have stood you in good stead in this kind of career.

Aanand: I think so. There's a lot in common, such as the canvassing skills in sales to what I think of as prospecting skills or canvassing skills in recruiting.

Marcia: If you have some advice for those who want to be in recruiting, what would you tell them, or what qualities should they have?

Aanand: I think it goes to that partner model that I believe in. Not a lot of managers are patient or willing to teach you their business so you have to earn that influence. You have to take those incremental wins, build a relationship and build influence. Some recruiters have the relationships but they never gain the influence. You have to understand their business but there are two sides to it: there's a back-end side and there's a front-end side. One side of it is being able to illustrate and analyze your work. Very few recruiters do analysis very well. You can look for efficiencies and you can look at: how many people do I screen, do managers screen, how many people get from the screen to an interview, or any sequence in the work flow and figure out where the problems lie and then improve. Not many recruiters can do that very well. They're not asked to at so many companies. On the backside of it, it's really learning and understanding the business, because in many cases the manager isn't going to help you discover the efficiency. You have to find it.

Marcia: What makes a good candidate, and what is it the candidate should avoid doing?

Aanand: I tell my friends, "network into companies." I think too many people make job changes as a knee-jerk reaction. There are very few resources out there that will help you understand what you're good at, what you're passionate about, where those overlap, what are the environments and lifestyles that you would enjoy and excel at, and what are the types of people that you want to surround yourself with. I think not enough candidates really do the introspective homework and then the market homework.

When you feel like you've done some introspection and some consultation with people, maybe a 360 of your own [review your own skills carefully], understand who you are, what you're good at, what you're passionate about, then figure out the industries and the companies based on the criteria that you've learned. Take that list of 10 companies and figure out how you can network into the decision-makers, regardless of whether they're hiring or not.

William Uranga

William has worked in retained search, as a contract recruiter, and is currently the Staffing Director at TiVo. I met him when he was a speaker at a professional organization talking about the science of recruiting and a quantifiable approach to the business.

William: I am the staffing director at TiVo in Alviso, California. I started recruiting about 15 years ago and it was something that I fell into. I didn't plan what I was going to do after college. I had a degree in political science since it was what I had always wanted to study, but beyond that I had not really planned how I was going to apply the degree. I didn't want to go into politics, or be a lawyer, and I didn't want to work in local government. I had an opportunity to do a couple of jobs – some of them involved nonprofit – and it was in one of the nonprofit organizations that I began recruiting summer interns. I learned a lot working in nonprofit. It was easy to recruit interns and the next thing I got to do was recruit volunteers for that same nonprofit. The challenge was that people were more willing to write a check and give it to the nonprofit than to donate their time, which was a much tougher sell. I was curious as to why it was like that and what could be done. That's how I got into recruiting and it broadened into general employment from there. I went from nonprofit into agency search, then I went in-house and came back into an agency.

Marcia: What's the difference between an in-house role and being an agency recruiter?

William: Historically there has been a big mindset difference. Retained search is one way of doing a search and another model is based on contingency. The contingency model tends to have much more of a transactional mindset, where the searchers are much more of a commodity item and you close [a candidate] when you can. I'm sure that would vary from agency to agency. There would be some recruiters who would take umbrage with that – they're very proud of their work. But certainly with the retained search – which is where my background is and I know much better than the contingency side – retained search is much more of a heavy investment in funds up front to be looking for a particular candidate and therefore the client's much more involved in the search process and expects much more information and client services, as do the candidates in that process. That seems to mirror a bit more closely what corporations want, as far as being an in-house recruiter, although I'm sure that varies too, because some companies are quite transactional. They have a lot of turnover and it becomes agency-like as far as getting the next set of bodies in.

I also think it depends on the company and the mandates of the executive team. If you're in-house the whole idea is to mirror the business practices of what the company's trying to do and make sure the staffing practices support that accurately. Here at TiVo we use all kinds of agencies – those that provide temporary help, those that provide permanent placement on a contingency model, as well as retained search. We tend to be a little more agnostic as far as the sort of firms that we use, as long as they are willing to work with us in our process.

Marcia: You've mentioned a lot of different forms of recruiting. How did you learn your skills?

William: I probably know the least about firms that operate in temporary and contingency since I do not have experience working inside them. I've worked with them across the table and to those that say that would color my view, I agree; it certainly would. I tend to be very driven, very analytical and I want to understand things and be able to shape things. The more I know, the more I'm able to communicate my client or my company's story and that tends to open up doors for other conversation as well.

I got into retained search almost by accident. I met somebody that was part of the BridgeGate group at a Starbucks and we did small talk and went from there. I didn't know beans from buckshot in that situation, but I did know I had to be doing a certain number of calls in order to get a certain number of responses. I focused on human resources at an executive level and some specialization. When you focus on a particular skill set, you start learning all the ins and outs. I focused within high technology, so the skill set was very specific, the market was very specific, so I got to know my sandbox very well. I got to see people's backgrounds as a result of resumes. Some came from agencies, some from consulting firms, and it was interesting to see what our firm's clients wanted: what would fit with their culture and skill sets and what they were trying to solve, and start correlating the two and be able to explain why our client was looking for this and why you as a candidate didn't fit or why you should consider it. At the same time in talking to the clients, I had to be well versed in this particular aspect of technology, so I was learning about software, middleware, tools, peripherals, chips, and biotech and what have you.

In order to do justice to your client, you've got to know their background, why they're a viable company, why this would be a good place to work and what you're going to learn from them. That means learning their elevator pitch and communicating in business terms, because often the company looking for candidates doesn't want to talk "HR-ese." They just had business problems, so we had to translate that into what experience an HR executive was going to need and provide an ideal candidate. I think that's usually the biggest challenge in HR, being the translator regarding business needs.

I had broad exposure and when I got in-house, I got to be a contract recruiter onsite with the company. I started to know people who were peers from agencies, contingency and what-have-you. I got to see some great experiences, some probably not so great, but I learned what business models work and who has their act together. Then, as a candidate myself, I got pretty savvy with what I was looking for in my next client. It's only really been in the last couple years that I have moved beyond being an individual contributor. There were some times in which I was frustrated and I wanted to move beyond just filling orders. But some of that was just being patient, knowing the right time or the right opportunity and being content and serving client groups or my boss's objectives and making sure they were being successful. I believed then and I certainly believe now that has its own rewards.

Marcia: How did you know it was the right time to move ahead and what kind of position did you obtain?

William: Well, probably the easiest decisions were when some of the decisions were made for me. I was laid off twice at two different companies for business reasons in which they were reducing their staffing or recruiting group down to one or two versus a half dozen, or it was a complete nuclearization of the whole department. If you knew the business model and the industry, you understood and knew it wasn't personal. I'm sure there are others who have had more unpleasant experiences and it was personal or political. Even if mine was, I'd choose not to believe that. At other times I was just assessing what I knew I needed to grow in next. After a while of being part of a search firm, I knew I wanted to see how the other side of the HR world operated. I didn't know if I'd necessarily like it or want to stay in it, but at least I'd be stronger in recruiting for knowing both sides and what the other side's concerns were and would do a better job in communication between the two.

I set out to learn and for some of these organizations it was being part of a team, learning how to work with others that had different strengths and specializations. For others maybe it was a start-up in which I was the jack of all trades, master of none, and I had to figure out how I was going to get it all done and put some processes in place to manage people.

Depending on what you'd like to do next, you should have some sort of game plan of A) know yourself and what environment, industry and profession you want to be in, and B) learning the next steps that will help get you there. I think probably one danger is to be in too much of a hurry to get a VP title. If that happens you may have the title, but you don't have the experiences to back that up. I've seen that in candidates across the board and I think the dot-com era exhibited some of that. I'd rather be a little slow in my career growth than topping out purely from the title standpoint and not having enough to round it out.

I don't think I've done anywhere near the amount of learning I still need to do. The biggest challenge of being internal with a company is you get so knee-deep in weeds that you forget to look up and do networking or self-education and learn from others. I try to make sure I do that not just for myself, but also bring my present team along, so they're better at communicating the company objectives and learning what's going on in recruiting and tools. If I'm not feeding myself in that sense, there's no way I'll have anything to give to anybody else. And part of that also leads to knowing when I need to move on.

Knowledge is a big key to a lot of different things. Let me start with simple stuff as far as language. I am very curious about how words and phrases get used and that translates into my writing and rewriting e-mails and other things. The better that I, or a member of my team, or a person can communicate their ideas, the farther we'll go, simply because people want to understand and respect a person or support them. I'm constantly reading.

From an industry standpoint, the latest technology is using a reader – an RSS [a way to publish or receive updated content such as blog entries, news headlines or podcasts]. The proliferation of blogs and news outlets is far too much for me to spend my day clicking from one website to another. I've leveraged one particular reader to have a lot of different feeds from logs and websites, so based on the titles that give me a good idea of what they're going to cover, and the ones that are of interest to me, I will read and/or pass along or share – either from a informational resource or an action item or tool – both for myself or for my team. That's one thing I do and you hear a lot as a result – conferences, training and what-have-you – and sometimes I am interested in going to those or encouraging my team members to go to. So that's just from the educational standpoint. I take classes as well.

Marcia: And you teach classes.

William: I do teach, so I give and I take in that sense. I teach at an extension of a local university.

The classes I take aren't necessarily HR-related. I took a recent class on project management. It gave me a different way of looking at things, because when people get raised in one particular discipline, sometimes the rest of the disciplines suffer from atrophy. I'm interested in how project managers – marketing or engineering – look at things. As a result, in recruiting specifically, you will have a start, you will have a process, you will have time, you will have resources and you will have a certain fixed dollar amount and it is a higher match made between the opportunity and an individual that's ready to take it on. I think it's very interesting to challenge whatever my assumptions were of how to do staffing in "an HR way."

I'm one of three people who report to our SVP and try to talk about common problems. If there's a problem in compensation, it is going to affect how I recruit and vice versa. We try to figure out if we need to do more training, if we need to do a better job in communicating via our intranet. Industry conferences have a huge role. The HR Symposium [in the Silicon Valley] is an excellent one to attend to see top thinkers. For recruiting, the Kennedy Center information and the ERE [a recruiting website at www.ere.net] tend to have very good thought leaders from a recruiting standpoint. Learn from them, take a shopping cart method: take what you can use, leave the rest for another time and as a result you will start rubbing shoulders with people. Sometimes there aren't things like that so it's good to teach what you do know. I think as a result [of teaching] I start to organize my thinking a little bit differently, and it's good to hear people specifically respond to what you're teaching.

One other thing that I would add is the importance of understanding the business. I try to go to conferences to learn what my marketing people are hearing and seeing. One thing most internal crews don't do well is understand competitive intelligence. What else are your competitors – whether it's in temp or talent – or the particular market segment are doing. You can read and certainly learn from other people, but as you interview, as you go to industry conferences, you hear what's going on and you can understand why sales is having a particularly tough year and what you can do about that. How does your current objective map to what you're hearing elsewhere in the market place?

The challenge in my situation of managing a team is that I am not focusing just on recruiting HR people, but I'm focusing on all kinds of skill sets and so for me it's a little tougher to know what's going on in marketing versus customer service versus engineering versus IT. That's where I'm trying to create "Mini-Mes" in the sense of recruiters, to be able to know what is going on and become industry experts.

Marcia: What do you hope to inculcate in the "Mini-Mes"?

William: I would say, one, a passion for the craft from a recruiting standpoint, and that means not just being good at recruiting but being well-rounded. Two, a person should have a thirst for understanding what is going on in the business. Even though they're contractors, they should know what's going on and why does my CEO think this way? How do I therefore translate that in culture and how do I determine whether this candidate is a fit for this culture? It's good to make sure that they're aligned with the hiring manager, but if it doesn't ultimately align with the CEO, you've just added more fuel to a bad fire instead of moving everybody in the same direction. The third thing is they should know what they've done and should be able to articulate what they've done. We have quarterly reviews when employees present a couple of slides of what they've done. I want them to know and not rely on the resume to carry them through. The fourth thing is that whenever it is an appropriate time for them to move on, they will have left a particular department or function in better shape than when they first got here. That's my mantra of giving back or beyond just filling the roles, and I'd say that they've had some fun doing it. It varies from culture to culture, but this is certainly one of those cultures that seek a more balanced lifestyle than grinding your contractor or employee into the ground for whatever short time you can get away with that.

Marcia: I do want to ask you about layoffs, because every recruiter who's been in the Valley for a while knows that there are those times. There are times like the depression that we went through recently where very few recruiters were working. You were working. How did you plan for that? What sustained you during that time?

William: Actually, I don't know that I planned well for it. In the dot-com bust I had a heads-up that it was coming. I mean, there was a major slow-down and 9/11 made it a no-brainer for everybody in many different industries. But I was able to stay with this company. In fact, I was the only staffing person that stayed on and the only reason I was able to do that was they realized they were able to use me in some HR roles. So there's one thing to be said: It's important not to be a one-trick pony in just staffing. It's good to develop other skill sets that are recognized and valued. I ultimately did get caught up in the fourth round of layoffs and it was what it was. I don't know that I had a plan B in that sense. Actually, I don't know many people that could.

I realize that a lot of people moved out of the area or went in totally different industries and are thinking about getting back into staffing – maybe only because there are not enough people to go around and find talent. But what I did to sustain myself during that time – which is part of your question – was I had to find some sort of contentment with what I did get. I did a little bit of retained search, I worked at a start-up, and I went and worked retail some of the time – something totally outside of recruiting. I had fun working some retail. It happened to be in an area of which I have a hobby and passion about. It was a nice switch but after a while it did get a little old. There's a different mindset and I found that they were certainly getting a lot out of me as far as the type of worker I am, while I was getting a lot of discounts. But beyond that, there wasn't anything that could really sustain me. I was really interested in being able to move back into a more full time position – not just in recruiting, but with one organization, and it happened over probably about a year.

I did have those days in which I had enough and thought I should move out of state, so I certainly don't want to make it sound like I had it all figured out. I had my moments of doubt but I stuck with it for a variety of reasons. Ultimately I had decided that if things were going to bounce back, it was likely to happen here much quicker than many of the other places I was considering in the U.S. and that turned out to be true. But there's no easy answer. I guess what keeps you sustained is that you're committed to that craft and you'll do almost anything within reason and legal means to stay in it.

Marcia: Do you have some advice for a new recruiter or someone thinking about going into the field?

William: The first thing I would say is get to know yourself as much as possible. Know what you're committed to – philosophically, what your interests are – and then really learn to be a student in that. It's one thing to get a paycheck for what we do, and I'll be the first to admit that's why I started working retail but it wasn't ultimately my goal. That's fine if it's a short term, but to be only doing it for the paycheck, or because it's what everybody said I was good at and should do, to me is only half the answer and I think that won't bear out in the long term.

Find out what you're really interested in, what sort of an environment you will work well in – maybe it is a contingency agency, maybe it is internal to a consulting firm or at a corporation, and then find out what industry makes sense for you. Maybe it is biotech, maybe service and hospitality, maybe manufacturing. They're all very different, they all have their moments of crisis as far as industry and the companies. Then within that learn your craft, be a sponge as much as possible, and learn – be educated, build your network, read and find people that are willing to invest their time in you so that you're better in your industry and craft.

Then I would say certainly turn around and start giving that back. The reason why you'll be able to give back is because you have been able to take on more than what you were originally assigned. I don't mean just more reqs. or physically to take on more things, but to be able to understand business – to understand why finance works the way it does, why the locale is the way it is – what idiosyncrasies in culture there are. Become expert in those areas so that you're able to help solve problems beyond just your aspect of the business and people will have a great appreciation because they depend on you. I think that would certainly provide advancement.

It may not be that these people want to advance, which is fine. We have people on this team that have done recruiting for 12 to 15 years and they don't want to get into management. They love what they do, they love the discipline and they love the skill set they recruit for. Give them the reqs client group and they're awesome at it, but don't ask them to manage a program or to manage people. That's not in them and I think it's important for people to know that.

At the same time, I think it's good to keep testing new theories, new ideas and new areas to grow in and not just because you're comfortable with them, but find out things that you're uncomfortable with, things you haven't done before, because as you keep pressing the envelope you find out more about yourself as a result.

Marcia: Every recruiter has stories about good candidates and those who could use improvement. Do you have some advice for candidates in general?

William: Yes, but I probably don't have enough time to go into them all. I'm at a company right now that is something on par with Kleenex in its industry. A lot of people know about it and I continue to be amazed that when people come in they only take that surface knowledge and they don't understand more about the company. They don't understand the executives. I'm not saying they should know VP level people, although we've had some of those, but even frontline individual contributors. I think a lot of people don't know what they're shopping for and as a result they either waste their time, my recruiter's time and the hiring manager's time. That's a big source of a disappointment; people just do not take time to study up about you as a possible place where they're going to invest a lot of their waking hours and energy. And it's not that they're not interested in the job, they just don't think outside of that. If you're with an agency and you put your candidate in front of your client and they haven't studied, it doesn't look good for them; it certainly doesn't make you look any better as a result.

I would say people are not ready to answer behavioral questions. Sometimes the people doing the interview don't even know how to ask them, so that's a double problem. When candidates are notified that we're looking for somebody to do X, Y and Z, and please give an example of when they've done, X-Y-Z, they often immediately go into theory and it will not earn them brownie points. It depends upon the environment, but here we look for people to wear a couple different hats. It could be that you market programs, but we're looking for somebody that also knows how to do reports and marketing analytics off the reports so they can develop better programs. The ability for somebody to ask questions about what's involved with this role and what they are going to be solving in a role usually doesn't come up. They should ask things like, "What am I supposed to do, who do I work with, what kind of resources?" They don't take it to the next level and ask what they are going to solve for the company and what should be a motivator when they come to any particular organization. I'd say those are a couple of things that people should ask but don't.

Marcia: Is there anything you'd like to add?

William: I think there's a big challenge out there. I was reading an article on Generation Y and the fact that a lot of people have to hop around. We're starting to see resumes that have one year here, one year there, maybe one and a half years elsewhere. The article said that the reason why people have to do this is because they have to pay off school loans and costs are going up. I'm not unsympathetic since I had to pay for the majority of my schooling. The challenge it's presenting for companies is that these people have not learned from their past experiences and it's hard to do that when you've been in a company for one year. You're typically learning the ropes and making a lot of mistakes the first year. The second year you're typically cleaning up the mistakes and by the third year you start hitting your stride and start to really contribute and be master of certain things. Those people are becoming far more a minority. I'm not sure what the solution is.

I would challenge those people to differentiate themselves far and above everybody else by sticking with their goals for a little bit longer and learn from them, rather than just hopping to the next job because they might have offered a few more coins. At this moment we have an employee or candidate driven market and just remember that we've been here before. During the dot-com days before the bust, people were switching horses all over the place and it is true in this day and age that the individual owns their career path more than any other generation before us. To that end that means you're also responsible for that. If you can take advantage of opportunities, the mistakes you make – you're going to need to somehow justify that down the road to another future employer, as was the case during the bust.

An employer has a choice: somebody that's been at a company for 3, 4, maybe 5 years, and somebody that's been hopping around for 1 year to 18 months. I think people are beginning to be careful about their career in the sense of where they are going next and what would be the things they're going to look for. Most people don't leave companies for monetary reasons. Make sure you know what the rest of the reasons are so when you entertain opportunities you make the smart decision that you'll be able to live with and that you'll be able to explain to future employers.

4

EXECUTIVE SEARCH

Mark Lonergan
Mark worked in sales and marketing and was recruited by a firm to join them as a retained search recruiter. His retained search business, Lonergan Partners, Inc. in Redwood Shores, California was established several years ago. Mark's professionalism and interview skills working with executives and board members made him an interesting interview subject. His website is www.lonerganpartners.com.

Mark: I'm the managing partner of Lonergan Partners based in Redwood Shores, where I retained an executive search firm focused on technology markets that primarily focused on doing searches for board-level directors, CEOs and people who report directly to the CEO.

Marcia: How did you get into this field?

Mark: I was the Vice President of Sales and Marketing at a public company in Minneapolis called ADC Telecommunications. I was placed there by a firm called Heidrick and Struggles. We went through a management changeover with the retirement of our chairman. About a year later I decided to leave, went back to Heidrick and Struggles and the next thing you know I ended up being a recruiter for them out here in the Silicon Valley.

Marcia: Did they train you?

Mark: Very much so. Heidrick believed then – and I'm not so clear what they believe now – that recruiting is an apprentice-ship process. So I got a lot of support and training from secretaries, other consultants, support staff, even training departments in order to help me learn how to do retained executive search.

I would say that typically the more senior the search that you're doing, the more likely it is that it's retained, which implies a level of trust in relationships before you begin a project. Oftentimes we rely on clients who've been clients of ours in the past to supply us with relationships going forward – board members, investors, CEOs, senior managers. In doing search for senior management the focus is on finding people with often very hard-to-find skills in terms of industry management capability, geographic skills in some cases, functional skills in others. It is incumbent upon the recruiter to be able to understand not only the requirements of the job, but the capabilities of the people that we're talking to.

Marcia: How do you screen your candidates' capabilities? It's one thing to understand what skills they've already amassed, but capability is different.

Mark: It's a good question. There are three or four things we do on a regular basis that seem to help. We break down people's requirements according to their core competencies, which necessarily means looking historically at what they've done well. Core competencies can include things like functional skill, management capability and strategic vision – issues that go beyond simple experiential components and go to issues about capability. And it's interesting – there are two answers to your question. As we do interviews, typically we interview our candidate for an hour and a half and we'll attempt to not only discover where they've been and what they're good at, but we'll also attempt to discover what they could be good at if given an opportunity. That necessarily means extrapolating what you've learned and exploring what's possible; that is a challenge sometimes.

Marcia: It's beyond going into behavioral interviewing; you're into a whole other realm. You're not really looking at what they've actually done as in "give me an example of when you did this."

Mark: Many of the people in our business do a remarkably poor job of understanding what people have done. There are certainly many recruiters who do an extraordinary job of behavioral interviewing, but they have to establish a baseline, and in our world that's what behavioral interviewing is. You need to find what tangible quantifiable skills and accomplishments are represented in the background and the capabilities of the person and then you begin that last bit of what they might be capable of doing in a different environment. Automatically you're extrapolating them into environments where they've not been. You ask yourself and your client the question: "What are they capable of doing?" If they do well at IBM, does that mean that they would do equally well at Unisys or some other company? How will they do with a different culture? How will they do with a different market, with a different set of products, with a different operational environment?

Those necessarily mean conjecture and extrapolation based on very careful evaluation and discussion with the individual. We often find that when it comes to what's possible, we get the best feedback, not from the candidate himself or herself, but often from the people that know them best – that have worked with them in the recent past. We call those "references," because people often are capable of providing color around what you already understand to be that person's capability.

Marcia: If you were interviewing a CTO, how many references might you call to complete the picture of this person?

Mark: Interestingly, one of the things we do that's different than others is we'll actually call two or three references before we introduce someone and then perhaps an additional six or seven after the project is nearing completion with one of our final candidates or final two candidates. It's a curious balance; you don't want to be intrusive, but at the same time you want to get interesting feedback. You do it up front, because oftentimes you can get answers to what I would describe as knowable challenges before the first interaction takes place. We're anxious to save everyone time and present people that seem to be closest to what our client had in mind. It's not unusual that during that discussion we'll discover things that make it clear that person can't contribute in the core competencies that we've laid out. We may truncate or even cut short an interview process as a result.

Marcia: What contributes to what you would call a top candidate? What qualities might that person have?

Mark: Remember, most of our candidates are going into positions of senior management. They often are dealing at second, third, or fourth level of management at a minimum.

Number one, it's often their management skills; their ability to identify, cultivate and develop quality individuals inside their teams that are capable of doing more for the company as time goes on. One of the best indications of that is the continued success that an individual's group may have long after that individual left, largely as a result of her or his ability to identify and cultivate great people. What we often describe as general management capability or functional management capability is really important. By the way, it doesn't always mean starting with new people; in fact it usually doesn't. It usually means cultivating the best of the people on the inside, along with the best of the people on the outside and looking for a team that is a much higher performer than it might be otherwise.

Other things: we look for tangible, credible success in the market, as identified – depending on the function – by success in market, product and financial results. We look for a track record of sustained success. The best people often have that and even in very tough markets are able to create really wonderful outcomes as a result of ingenuity, creativity and skills that sometimes they don't even know they have.

A good example: in the telecom market, many companies have been very challenged over the last four or five years. It's been a very tough market and yet consistently, the best managers in that market seem to come out with very good results. They may not be what they had envisioned in '97 and '98, but some of the very best companies were actually most actively built in the toughest part of the telecom market.

We look for that sustainable track record of success, which brings with it confidence and an intellectual component. Most of the people who do very well over long periods of time are not just more creative, they think harder about the problems and they anticipate better than some of their counterparts.

Marcia: There's probably a lot from your sales and marketing background that serves you well in this kind of a role – that you understand what the products are and how to present the products – the products being both the client company and the candidate or potential candidate.

Mark: It can be a good background for what we do here. I temper it a bit: there are a lot of people in the search business who come out of sales and marketing backgrounds. Equally, I see extraordinary people come out of HR backgrounds, engineering backgrounds and financial backgrounds.

What seems to be more important is a person's ability to form and sustain a relationship. It's not always easy to have relationships with people where you're able to share honesty, integrity, and you're able to be straightforward with them about the challenges you're confronting. Some salespeople find that very difficult. It's much easier for some sales people in our world to become so focused on what I'll call "finishing a project." They sometimes forget that finishing a project doesn't happen with the placement of an individual, it happens two or three years after an individual has been placed and he or she has had great success in that job.

I've seen people from stock brokerages, lawyers and software engineers become dynamic, thoughtful consultants to management. I've seen people who have very extraordinary experience – academic and consulting experience – not do as well, because they are more challenged to be consultative with their clients.

Marcia: Do you find a difference between recruiting for somebody who's a CEO or CFO – anybody at C-level, vs. a board member? Is there a difference in the way that you approach the person?

Mark: Board searches are some of our favorite work and often we're looking for board members who are the first non-investor members for companies that we get involved with, and that has a great deal of pleasure associated with it, because often they have a discreet capability that's unlike anyone else who's previously been involved in the board, except for perhaps operating management.

The difference is that the board member, if you think about it, is often motivated not by financial gain, but by his or her willingness and ability to add value and create value where perhaps value needed to be created. In a functional position, like the chief marketing officer, it's a job. And it's a job that they take very seriously from an operational standpoint. But let's be clear: most of them still cash paychecks and need those and they look at it as part of their career. So those people tend to be much more operational, more tactically adept, they tend to be more focused on their functional specialty if they're not a CEO or a general manager. The board member tends to be more of a generalist, a strategist, a consultant to senior management and often a sounding board.

Marcia: Could you talk about the role of your personal network in building up your business and your clientele?

Mark: In our world, personal network is built on trust - period. Everything else in a personal network is ancillary to that number one rule. The personal network, from my client standpoint, says that if we trust Mark and his people well enough we'll give them additional projects, we'll trust them to get our project done well and on time and thoughtfully.

In a candidate context, it means that I trust that if I'm going to raise my hand and demonstrate an interest in a confidential project, that I trust Mark and his firm will be able to maintain a confidence, will be able to demonstrate real knowledge of the company and the opportunity, will be straightforward with me about what it is that I am looking at, and there won't be any surprises.

The extent to which we're able to build a sustainable personal network is usually a function of our ability to create trust, to create a conduit of information, both for the client and for the candidate.

Our network is nothing more than a compilation of all of the interactions that we've had for almost six years that we've been doing this. I've known people in the search business – I've been here for almost 15 years – for a long, long time. As long as they continue to trust us, believe in us, believe that we'll be honest, thoughtful, that we'll understand those areas where they need the most help, then we'll continue to build that trust relationship and therefore our network.

Marcia: Do you have some advice for someone considering getting into retained search as a career?

Mark: My personal advice is that this is not something that I would recommend to anyone before they've been in a career doing something else for the first 10 years. The reason is that if you're going to be asked to find a vice president of sales, even for a very young company, you're going to call upon every skill that you ever learned in a functional specialty – every management skill, every nuance of your training – to be able to help you understand what it is that the client's trying to accomplish and what it is that the candidates are going to want to know more about.

The result is that the people who will do best in our business are often people who came in during their late twenties and early thirties – people who've had an opportunity to work at Apple, at IBM, at Booz Allen Hamilton and at Goldman Sachs and have taken all of the skills and experiences and translated them over here. There are other people who land in our business much earlier than that. Unfortunately for many of them it's very difficult to begin in a support role – an associate's role – in many of the larger firms and ultimately become a full-fledged consultant and partner.

Ironically, you may do better entering our business as a consultant from Apple than with seven years at a top four firm in our business. That's a bit controversial, but often our hiring clients will complain that they've got people who don't understand their business who are trying to conduct searches that they don't understand as well.

If your real interest over the longer term is to do retained searches in the financial services business, my advice would be spend seven or eight years as the market leader in the financial services world and then make your move armed with the experience and the capabilities that you've been taught.

Marcia: Do you have some advice for candidates?

Mark: The best candidates are the ones who understand information exchange and the trust relationship. The best candidates tend to be thorough, responsive, and honest, even on issues that sometimes don't reflect as well on them. They tend to be clear-spoken about what their requirements are. They tend to be very circumspect about their ability to fit a situation that's been presented to them. They tend to be very open to considering ideas, but very honest about being able to evaluate their talents versus the ones that are being proposed.

In the search business it universally seems to be true that some of our favorite candidates are the ones who, as a function of your interaction, will quickly decide that they're not going to engage in a search. That's a good thing because what it tells us is they're very clear about what it is they'd like to hear the next time they get contacted by our firm. We tend to solicit that information and listen for it carefully, and those are the candidates that quite often are contacted by us with something much closer to what they had in mind.

I think this really is about the marriage; it's not about the wedding. This is about finding a home where both parties – both the hiring firm and the individual – are delighted with the outcome and there were no surprises. It is where even the known flaws were examined and understood ahead of time and the candidate understands his or her role in that. Know that no one is perfect, that a candidate tends to be very direct about: "I have real concerns about these two areas, I don't see that there's a fit there – thank you very much, but I'm going to pass." It could range everything from the culture that they encounter, the management style that they're asked to examine and the geography.

There's an old saying in our business that you can't sell geography; it either fits or it doesn't. The right candidates are usually very good about saying, "I'm sorry – I live in Orange County, I'm not prepared to accept a CEO position in a place like the Bay Area, that isn't going to work for myself and my family, thank you very much, here are the things I'd like to hear about the next time you call." We tend to get a lot of value from those candidates; not only do we learn a lot more about the company that we're representing, but we also hear a lot more about when we should be in contact with them next.

One final thing – I think everybody who's done this for a long time will tell you this – the best candidates have a very clear picture of what they'd like to find in their next opportunity. The best candidates tend to narrow the field considerably based on functional area, industry, market, geography, income – they tend to be very clear-spoken on those issues. It's those candidates who often get the most interest from firms like ours.

The ones who are the least focused and the most diffuse in terms of their expressed interests are likely to be seen as much more confused and therefore less likely to be a fit for something that we're trying to bring to them. If I had one bit of advice it would be think hard before that phone call about what it is that you'd like to encounter and be consistent with what those requests actually turn into.

In the best of all worlds – and I would say this is true of all recruiters, but especially in the retained world – we should – and I think the best of us do – pattern ourselves more after doctors than sales people. A doctor is prepared to do a thorough diagnostic, to give some careful interaction with a patient and to work jointly with that patient to come to a treatment program when one is required, in order to affect the best outcome. The best recruiters try to do exactly the same thing, even if sometimes that treatment program means a bit of pain or a bit of discomfort for both parties involved.

The best of us, I would hope – and I would certainly like to put myself in that group – understand that their responsibility doesn't end with the completion of the project; it only starts with the completion of the project and it only ends when you've had significant time and you've had a chance to see how that person performs. We do best when we speak most clearly, thoughtfully and consultatively to both clients and the people in our networks.

Toby Freedman

Toby has worked in business development in a biotech form and is an executive (retained) search recruiter in her own agency, Synapsis Search, specializing in the life sciences (biotech) industry. She recently wrote a book about careers in biotechnology and career development to be published in 2007. Her website is www.synapsissearch.com.

Toby: I received my PhD in molecular biology, then I did two post-docs and joined a start-up company. I was on the business side and during that time I had three CEOs in three years. They were all really good CEOs, but none of them had the right background so we didn't get VC [Venture Capital] funding. That brought home how important management is in the sciences. Obviously you need really good technology to be a successful company, but you also need good management. That's why I got into executive search and I joined a firm that exclusively dealt with life sciences where we did mostly VP to COO [Vice President to Chief Operations Officer] level searches for emerging biotech companies and medical device companies. I did that for three years and I loved it; it was great fun.

During that time I became frustrated with the number of calls from people that needed career advice. There really isn't a good book out there that explains the different career opportunities in the biotechnology industry, because it's so deep and vast and there are so many opportunities – it's more than you might imagine. I decided to write a book about careers in biotechnology and career development, which hopefully is going to be published by the end of this year. After the primary writing was finished I started my own search firm called Synapsis Search and I specialize in Life Sciences. I developed my own business model which is unique; people seem to like it and things are going well.

Marcia: Tell me a little bit about your change from working at a start-up to working in executive search. Were you trained when you went into search? How did you decide to go into search? That's such a switch in your career.

Toby: That was a radical switch. When I was working in the start-up, people were calling me all the time since I'm just super-networked, saying, "I need help and we're hiring XYZ, can you help me?" I was referring people and I thought, I'm doing this for free anyway, I might as well get paid for it; so that was part of the picture. The other part was a realization that people with a background like mine, with a deep knowledge in science or medicine, can do quite well in executive search firms. It's quite fun because you're dealing with executives and venture capitalists and leading scientists and you really get to know everybody; you get to know the landscape, get to know the latest news about companies and how companies are doing. It's a high level view of your own specific industry.

I really enjoy being in an executive search firm. Making that transition wasn't that bad because I had the right personality and the right background for that. I was in the business-development world and that's a great parlay into executive search. The more contacts you have the better and if you really network, it's a lot easier. When I joined the executive search firm there really wasn't any bona fide training; it was sort of on-the-job training where they had me work on a search with people and it wasn't that hard to pick up. I didn't get official training from a top five search firm so I don't know what that entails. Interestingly enough the best recruiter in the company I was in (in life sciences) was a guy who got a college degree and went straight into recruiting. He was fast, quick and really good and he didn't have a science background at all.

Marcia: Was your on-the-job training listening to him and other recruiters and trailing them, or how did that work?

Toby: It wasn't so difficult. I could speak the language of the life sciences; it was pretty simple to call people and when I'd run into situations where I didn't know how to handle it I could then ask people. When you're interacting with people and you're dealing with jobs, there're a million different scenarios that can come up and there's no way you can anticipate them. You need to work through them and once you have experience doing it then it's easier the next time around. There're a lot of ethical issues and even now in my own search firm I run into that. I have to think about things and really make the right call. It's difficult.

Marcia: What would be an example of an ethical issue you would face?

Toby: There are ethical issues any time that you are dealing with people's jobs and livelihoods. Every time a candidate interviews, they risk the chance of being seen and someone in their company may find out.

Marcia: You mentioned starting your own search firm. Is it the same kind of search?

Toby: I'm trying to specialize in middle-management in the life sciences. When I worked in the retained search firm it was mostly VP to CEO level. I want to go into middle management because there are a lot of really good executive search firms. It's very competitive and there are just amazingly good people out there with a large network and they've been doing it for many years and they're very good. Then there're a lot of temp-to-hire search firms because they're also very good, but there are not a lot of people in the middle management world. That, to me, was the easiest entry because it's the least competitive. The other areas are already populated with very good, competent people. Middle management is where I'd like to go but I've done everything from research associates to COO in the short time that I've been recruiting on my own. Every search is difficult – but it's going well.

Marcia: Do you have some advice for people who are interested in going into recruiting?

Toby: There are a couple things: First thing - you really need to know your industry. Biotech is really specific and I can't tell you how many calls I got from recruiters who had no clue. Credibility is everything in this field. When I was working at a start-up, people were calling me for CFO [Chief Financial Officer] positions. I don't know anything about accounting or finance and they were calling me and they wanted something in some other therapeutic area that I didn't even work on. Obviously, I'm not going to give them the time of day because they don't know what they're talking about. It's worse with the scientists, because they're really, really selective.

The top talent gets calls from recruiters all the time and they're very coveted and hard to call. They're not going to return your calls if it's clear you don't know what you're talking about. I would recommend first getting to know your industry and getting to know it well, because you need to know what companies are doing what, who the major players are and that'll save you so much time.

For example, if you're working for a cancer company- and in the biotech world there're lots of companies but only a small fraction work on cancer- so you're wasting your time going to all these other companies and trying to recruit. You have to get to know the industry that you're in.

Biotech is a really difficult field, so I wouldn't recommend that one [as an entry into recruiting]. The life sciences are really fun but the biotech world is really complicated, so I might recommend other areas such as accounting that is good no matter where you go. There're some areas where you can be in any industry, but definitely get to know the field.

Marcia: Do you have advice for candidates? Every recruiter sees things that they should do and should not do.

Toby: One thing that you should never, ever do is sidestep the recruiter. I've had that happen to me and I really hate it. You present a candidate and they don't trust you and then they bypass you and contact your hiring manager. Then the hiring manager will forward the e-mail to me and then I don't trust the candidate after that because it's insulting. My enthusiasm for their candidacy goes down greatly!

Let's say you were applying for a job at Genentech. It is much better to send it to the hiring manager than it is to the HR department, because the HR department may not know where to send your resume and so you may not get your resume where you want it to go.

It's true that, yes, it's better to bypass the recruiter when you first make your initial introductions – it's better to do that, because the recruiter may not get there. But once you've initiated a conversation with a recruiter and they present you as a candidate, you should not bypass them because you're basically destroying your relationship with them.

Referrals are the best way to get into a company – not a recruiter. In my industry they did a survey and found 65 percent of employees got their job through networking and a very few got their jobs from recruiters. Don't rely on recruiters to get you a job, that's for sure.

Candidates network, they go to meetings, they talk to people, they say, "I have a background in blah-blah-blah, and I'm looking for a job in this." Somebody will then say, "Oh, I know so and so, you know, call this person." That's how it happens.

Marcia: How do you build your network?

Toby: Every industry's different so it depends on what industry you're in. I'm in the biotech world so I can only speak to that. I go to all the biotech meetings in the Bay Area and I'm on the board for several programs. I'm on the program committee too, so I'm always inviting speakers to speak at events. If you go to enough meetings and hear people talk, you get to know a lot of people.

I network as much as possible. I keep business cards that I put into a book and currently I'm on my sixth one – it's a binder. I keep them and then I have a database and when they're really important contacts I'll stick them in my database.

Marcia: Do you have any further thoughts you'd like to share?

Toby: There was something about another mistake candidates make. There's some weird assumption that a person is going to work with one recruiter who will get them a job. It's just totally backwards. If a recruiter happens to have a search open and the candidate has the right background, the recruiter then can help you get a job, but otherwise they can't. They need to work with as many recruiters as possible whom they trust and then also network themselves and try to get their own jobs. Don't rely on recruiters to get you a job.

GLOSSARY

- A -

Agency Recruiter – Recruiter working at an agency. Companies sub-contract job orders and pay 20-30 percent of the new hire's first year base salary. Usually no exclusive relationship with the company and are only paid when the candidate begins work at the company.

ATS – Applicant Tracking System – program used to track candidates

- C -

CFO – Chief Financial Officer

COO – Chief Operations Officer

CTO – Chief Technical Officer

Consultant – Individual hired for a short term project.

Contingency Recruiter – see "Agency Recruiter"

Contract Recruiter – Professional recruiter hired for a short term project to focus on filling requisitions.

Corporate Recruiter – Recruiter is an employee of the company and tasked with finding, qualifying, and shepherding new employees for the corporation.

- F -

FAA – Federal Aviation Administration

Flip Searcher, Flip Recruiter, Flippers – Recruiters who find candidates exclusively via
Internet searching.

- I -

In House Recruiter – see "Corporate Recruiter"

IPO – Initial Public Offering, the first sale of private stock to the public

- H -

Headhunter – see "Agency Recruiter"

HRCA – Human Resources Consultants Association

HRIS – Human Resources Information System, a database for corporate Human Resources Departments

Human Resources – "HR" professional works for a company. Duties may be specific as in Recruiter, or be general, as in a "Generalist". Scope of duties vary and may include recruiting, compensation, benefits, training, coaching, employee relations, labor relations, organizational design and development, legal compliance and reporting.

-N-
NCHRA – Northern California Human Resources Association

-O-
Outplacement – services including resume writing and interview skills coaching to help people who have been laid off

- P -
PHR – Professional Human Resources –certification earned through the HRCI
PTS – Prospect Tracking System – program used to track prospective candidates
Profiler – Researched name of possible candidate is provided to a profiler. Profiler calls potential candidate and does a brief telephone screen, learning about job title, duties, brief description of employment history, education, salary and interest level in new position.

- R -
R&D – Research and Development
REQ – Job requisition, an opening budgeted and approved by the corporation.
Researcher – Recruiter or firm first analyzes the industry, compiles a list of competitors, breaks down the organization chart and creates a list of names of potential candidates.
Retained Search – Company is hired exclusively to find top candidates typically for executive positions. Retained search companies are paid a portion of their fee upfront (usually 33-35% of base salary target), another percentage paid in 3-6 months, and the balance paid when the search is over.
Ruse – An invented story used to bypass "gatekeepers" such as receptionists in order to contact a potential candidate.

- S -

SHRM – Society for Human Resources Management (international organization)

Sourcer – see "Researcher"

Spec – Job or candidate specifications.

- T -

Third Party Onsite – Agency representative works onsite at a client's location doing payroll services for temporary workers, finds and reviews resumes, manages third party temporary workers from vendors such as Kelly Services or Manpower.

- V -

VC – Venture Capital, a company or individual with private equity (funds) investing in new businesses

RESOURCES

ERE – recruiting news, information and community
www.ere.net

HR Symposium – annual event in the Silicon Valley
www.hrsymposium.com

HRCA – Human Resources Consultants Association
www.hrca.com

HRCI – Human Resources Certification Institute – internationally recognized certifying body for the HR profession   www.hrci.org

NCHRA –Northern California Human Resources Association
www.nchra.org

SHRM – Society for Human Resources Management (international organization) www.shrm.org

Silicon Valley Women in Human Resources...and Friends
www.ourhrsite.com

About Marcia Stein, PHR

I am a Human Resources Consultant, Contract Recruiter, and Preventing Sexual Harassment Trainer. I offer a variety of training programs and am a professional speaker and moderator for organizations, businesses and job search groups.

I have extensive experience as a Human Resources Manager, at times the sole practitioner in several small companies, and have also worked as a Contract Recruiter and Staffing Manager in the Silicon Valley. My experience also includes work as a Career Transition Consultant working with job search groups and private clients.

I earned a PHR (Professional Human Resources, a national certification earned through the HRCI) and have a Bachelor's Degree from Virginia Commonwealth University. I also founded a networking and mentoring group for women in HR in the Silicon Valley.

To contact me, please send email to mstein@ourhrsite.com or write to me at:

Marcia K. Stein, PHR
c/o WJT Bashamer Publishing
10156 Camberley Lane
Cupertino, CA 95014

QUICK ORDER OR REQUEST FORM

The most efficient and least expensive way to fulfill a request or an order is via email. The book and articles are available in PDF format and can be ordered at ourhrsite.com. You may request information by using this form.

Email: mstein@ourhrsite.com
Fax: 206-350-1969

Mail: WJT Bashamer Publishing, Marcia Stein
        10156 Camberley Lane, Cupertino, CA 95014 USA

Please send the following articles sent via email as Adobe PDF files. I understand that I may return any of these products for a full refund for any reason, no questions asked.

TITLE

_____

_____
_____
_____

Please send more FREE information on:

☐ Books   ☐ Articles   ☐ Mailing Lists
☐ Consulting   ☐ Speaking/Workshops   ☐ Other
☐ How to tell YOUR story

Name: _____
Address: _____
City: _____
State/Zip: _____
Country: _____
Telephone: _____
Email: _____

RECEIVE A FREE ARTICLE VIA EMAIL!

Because you have purchased a copy of my book, you may request **one free article** *posted on my website. Please review current articles on the website at ourhrsite.com/WJT_Shop.html and use this form to order the free article of your choice.*

Email: mstein@ourhrsite.com
Fax: 206-350-1969

Mail: WJT Bashamer Publishing, Marcia Stein
         10156 Camberley Lane, Cupertino, CA 95014 USA

Please send my free article via email. The article I'd like to receive is: _____.
I understand that the article will be sent via email in Adobe PDF format.

Please send FREE information on:

☐ Books   ☐ Articles   ☐ Mailing Lists

☐ Consulting ☐ Speaking/Workshops ☐ Other

☐ How to tell YOUR story

Name: _____

Email: _____

Please double-check your email address. If it isn't clearly written, I may not be able to fulfill your request.

I'd like to be added to your email list.

☐ Yes, please add me to the list for updates.

☐ No, thank you. I do not wish to be added to the email list.

www.ingramcontent.com/pod-product-compliance
Lightning Source LLC
Chambersburg PA
CBHW032304210326
41520CB00047B/1212